The background design and colours on the front and back covers of this book are those used on the flag of the Corps of Royal Engineers. They are said to symbolise two pontoons in a river of blood.

Books by this author

Sapper to Subaltern : Two Years National Service
1957-1959

A Personal Journey

* * * * *

Technology of the Ancients : An Overview

To order any of these books go to **www.lulu.com** and type the title of the book, or, the author's full name, into the **Search Bar** and follow the links.

Credit Card or PayPal

These books are only available online

Sapper to Subaltern
Two Years National Service

1957-1959

A Personal Journey

Charles M G Husband

Published December 2015

DEDICATION

To Lorna and our girls; Stephanie, Kirsty & Vicki

GLOSSARY

Within the text there may be some abbreviations, words and phrases that are unfamiliar to the general reader. These have been defined within the **GLOSSARY** at the end of this book.

ACKNOWLEDGEMENTS

After I decided to write up the personal history of my national service years I started to trawl the furthest regions of my memory for stories, facts, and all else besides, to enliven the text. It was then that I found that at this remote distance in time from my two years service in the army, the memory can play nasty tricks with what you think happened and what actually happened. However, in this respect I have been most fortunate in that during those two years I had written a number of letters home to Lorna (girl friend, fiancée and wife) and that to my surprise I found that she had kept those very letters. Likewise, I had kept all the letters she had written to me. In addition, sparse as they were, I also had diaries from that period. Furthermore, our attic turned out to be a bit of a treasure trove in respect of photographs and other memorabilia - things I had long forgotten about. So, with all this documentation and other miscellaneous items, I have been able to prepare a reasonably good and accurate calendar of all the events recorded in this slim volume. However, good as this documentation was, there were many facts that I could not remember and in this respect I have been greatly assisted by Ian Chappell. It was when carrying out an Internet search for some forgotten facts and figures I chanced upon Ian's name as someone who had also served at Guillemont Barracks, my main army base during my two years national service. After contacting him I discovered that he had been Chief Clerk in 'B' Squadron some nine months or so before I had arrived and he very kindly agreed to supply me with all the bits of information that he could remember from his time there. That has been of huge assistance to me and it helped me galvanise my enthusiasm to start and finish this personal project. I'm also indebted to Patrick Watson, a fellow cadet through our officer cadet training for his recollections of his service in Germany. And, of course, I'm greatly indebted to my old buddy - Rusty - whose memory helped me regarding many an exploit.

I'm also indebted to my friend Andrew Muir, who was a national service sapper in Korea during the Korean War (1950-1953) and who was able to enlighten me regarding his service in that 'hell hole'.

Contained within the photographs at the end of this book I have included a few that were taken by Messrs Reader & Ward, the firm that supplied photographic services to the army in the Aldershot Garrison Area during the 1950s and 1960s. I have done my very best to locate this firm to seek their permission to reproduce the aforementioned photographs, but to no avail. It would appear that they have ceased trading because I could find no trace of them. If they are still trading I offer my apologies for failing to track them down and obtain their permission for publication of the photographs.

I am further indebted to Ian Chappell for granting me permission to reproduce his photograph of the Regimental Headquarters of 3TRRE

I also wish to express my gratitude to Mr Andrew Orgill, Senior Librarian at the Royal Military Academy Sandhurst, for his help in answering my request for information regarding the former Mons Officer Cadet School in Aldershot.

CONTENTS

INTRODUCTION

Where to begin and why bother? These were the questions that inevitably arose when deciding whether or not to write up this personal history; but then again, why not? Undoubtedly, there would be a considerable effort needed to achieve my goal, and much research as well - but it could all be a bit of fun, as well as a challenge. And did anyone in the family know about these experiences, or even care about them? Possibly not, indeed, probably not; but nonetheless I felt that they should be recorded. A bit of our family history if nothing else, and so much family history goes unrecorded. The family probably knew I had been in the Royal Engineers at one time, but not much else. So I made the decision - 'go for it'.

And it has been fun. Along the way I have made contact with Ian Chappell whom I have mentioned earlier. Ian has been of great assistance in jogging my memory about many of the physical aspects of Guillemont Barracks where we both served at various times. It was also clear from the information that Ian provided to me, that between mid 1957 and early 1958 there had been a large turnover in the permanent staff at Guillemont Barracks; particularly within Regimental Headquarters and 'A' & 'B' Squadrons. This is a pertinent fact that needs to be borne in mind if former personnel try to compare their service and experience within these squadrons when they were there. As a consequence, the tales and experiences that I am about to relate are but 'a snapshot in time'.

The Training Brigade of the Royal Engineers, of which 3 Training Regiment Royal Engineers (3TRRE) where I served most of my time, was one of four regiments involved in the training of sappers before they entered service with another RE regiment. No. 3TRRE comprised three squadrons. 'A' & 'B' Squadrons who were the training squadrons for the regiment, and 'C" Squadron which was the administrative arm of the regiment that organised and ran the life of the camp from cookhouse and stores, to military transport, and all other matters needed to keep a regiment functioning. And there was also the small group known as Regimental Headquarters (RHQ) comprising the Commanding Officer (CO), the Second in Command (2IC), the Adjutant the Regimental Sergeant Major (RSM) and the Regimental Chief Clerk.

'A' and 'B' Squadrons each comprised three parties, or troops, as they are also known. These parties were the sappers undergoing sapper training and, depending upon the time of year and the exodus from universities, colleges and schools, could each number between 60-100 sappers. In that respect they contained a greater number of soldiers than would normally be found in a troop in the field. Training consisted of two parts; infantry training and military engineering. Infantry training consisted of weapons training with rifles and Bren guns, not forgetting the inevitable foot drilling on the parade ground and weapons warfare, including bayonet practice. Military engineering consisted of all aspects of sapper engineering covering everything from mine warfare, explosives handling and demolitions, to Bailey bridging and watermanship. The sapper engineer had to be versatile, use his initiative, and be able to turn his hand to anything and everything.

The experiences of national servicemen are as varied as the grains of sand on a beach. Each one has a different story to tell - some immensely boring, and others more dangerous than they would have cared for. But there was no doubting the fact that those servicemen that ambled along, skiving as much as possible, had the most boring experiences, or non-experiences, with many leaving disaffected after two years of wasted service.

Within my own close group of friends who served as national servicemen within the Royal Engineers, one friend, Andrew, previously mentioned, served as a sapper during the Korean War (1950-1953) and has many traumatic memories of that engagement. Another, David, served as a second lieutenant in Movement Control in the early 1950s within the London

Garrison Area, and was responsible for the movement of troops within that region, from sappers to generals. Undoubtedly, this was a 'plum' posting since he could live at home in London for most of the time. I think it is now the case that The Royal Logistics Corps carry out this function. A third colleague, Ian, was posted to Tripoli, again in the early 1950s and rather enjoyed his time there as a second lieutenant in a field regiment. Patrick (commissioned at the same time as myself) was posted as a second lieutenant to a field regiment in Germany; not always a great posting because of the long periods of boredom between training exercises. Nevertheless, it had its moments, as the Russians were not being particularly friendly at this time. Another colleague, David, was posted as a second lieutenant to an Assault Engineer Regiment in the south of England to be on stand by for overseas duty at very short notice. A sapper had to be versatile – 'a jack of all trades'. But Training Brigade where I was posted also had its moments. As an officer one had the opportunity to fire everything from Bren guns to Sten guns, rifles to pistols, and all else in between, notwithstanding the opportunities that came along to blow up a few 'bits and bobs'. The downside was that within the training squadrons it was 'bull' all the way. Nothing could ever be just OK; everything had to be 'on the ball'. There was no other option. But it was not all 'bull'. Just as much fun was the experiences of non-military escapades. Thus, it was a relatively easy decision to put 'pen to paper' and record the good and the bad, if for no other reason than it was part of my personal history.

One consequence of service as a commissioned officer during national service was that on demob you were immediately transferred to the Regular Army Reserve of Officers (RARO) for recall in the event of mobilisation. In my case I was notified that I was promoted to first lieutenant on the 31st. January 1960 and that I would remain on the RARO list until June 1974 or until age 45, whichever was the earlier? In the early 1950s this also entailed a two-week Territorial Army camp for a refresher course; but later in the 1950s this requirement was discontinued. I do not know what the requirements were for other ranks.

1957

A Good Year, maybe…

This was a good year by most standards, maybe…
I had completed all my studies, including my final exams in the early spring leaving the later spring and summer free for socialising. These were glorious seasons. Every available hour not engaged with working and the necessities of life were spent with Lorna, my girl friend of some many months. And by every hour that is what I mean. We would meet after work and spend time together, and, according to the diaries from these days a great deal of the time was spent in Inverleith Park, Edinburgh - our home city. When carrying out the research for this little book, Lorna (now my wife) was won't to say - "but what did we do in the park". Now let me think … If not in the park, or dancing, or at the 'flicks', then we could be found in the flat near to the park, which she shared with her twin sister and another girl friend.

The memories of the sitting room in that flat keep flooding back. The chaise longue with its slightly prickly fabric covering, and the squeaky floorboards; those damned squeaky floorboards. The decibels emanating from those floorboards appeared to grow in intensity as the lateness of the hour wore on. Would I wake the owner of the flat who lived on the floor below as I made a late, or was it an early, exit? That was always a concern.

More often than not I would take my leave in the early hours of the morning, and since I lived more than three miles away, and had to walk home, I soon became on nodding terms with the milkman as he delivered the milk to our tenement flat. Sleep was often in short supply and soon I became inured to surviving on very little, but at least I was enjoying life. This facility for surviving on little sleep was to stand me in good stead in later months, although I did not know it at the time.

But a pall hung over those carefree days. A dark cloud was slowly rising over the horizon - something that could not be ignored. I had been deferred national service for five years whilst I completed all my college studies, but now at last I could be deferred no longer. Two years serving 'Betty Windsor' beckoned.

And so it was that sometime in the late spring or early summer I received the dreaded letter from the War Office, and, as I recall, I was offered a choice of which service I wanted to enter. Without much hesitation I selected the RAF, but only if it could be aircrew - I did so much want to be a pilot. A desire flamed by reading the exploits of *The Dam Busters* on their various missions. Sometime later, and after much correspondence, I was told that I could enter the RAF and enter the selection process for aircrew. I was over-joyed. This delight was, however, short-lived. Not long afterwards I received yet another communication informing me that the rules had changed and that for me to enter the selection process I would have to enlist for a Short Service Commission of three years. Thus my dreams were grounded; I was not prepared to serve for this extended period of time. This rejection did however give me the opportunity to request that I be enlisted in the Royal Engineers, a service for which I felt I was reasonably well qualified having completed five years of study in civil engineering. And so in the late summer I received the usual buff coloured envelope requesting that I attend a 'medical' at Dean Park House, Edinburgh. I arrived in advance of the appointed hour and although it was summer everything in that building seemed to be cold, including the temperature - or perhaps it was just nerves. As I had anticipated, medically, every thing was 'A Okay'; so there was no way out. Before long I would have to take the 'Queen's Shilling'. At this time two other close friends and colleagues received their summonses so it seemed we would all be going together.

The challenge of the unknown future lay ahead.

1TRRE, Merebrook Camp, Malvern, Worcestershire

Some weeks later I received the dreaded letter from the War Office inviting me [sic], at Her Majesty's' pleasure' to attend Merebrook Camp, Malvern, Worcestershire, home of 1 Training Regiment Royal Engineers (1TRRE) on Thursday 10 October 1957. Coincidentally, one of my friends Don received his papers requesting his attendance some weeks after me, and Jimmy, the third of our trio, requesting his attendance some considerable time after that. Nothing daunted, Jimmy immediately contacted the appropriate authorities requesting an earlier 'call-up' so that we could all be together - or so he assumed. His wish was granted, but in the weird and wonderful ways of the authorities he was assigned to the Royal Artillery - this was not what he had wanted - and there was no way out. Bye bye Jimmy! With the benefit of experience, even if we had all been posted to 1TRRE on the same day it is highly unlikely that we would ever have served together at any time, such were the vagaries of national service.

And so the day dawned. Well, not quite! Malvern was a considerable way from Edinburgh, and to get there on time meant a late night departure from Waverley Station and a couple of changes of train en-route. Armed with the travel warrant that had been so generously provided and a minimum of clothing, I set off from a cold and mist shrouded Waverley Station with the air heavy with the smoke and fumes from the old steam locomotives. Lorna was barely holding back the tears and I certainly felt no better. With hindsight it felt somewhat like a scene from *Brief Encounter.* What lay ahead one wondered? Actually, what horrors lay ahead would have been more appropriate?

Which Malvern, was it Little Malvern or Great Malvern, I remember not, but it mattered little, there was nothing to see. Mist, or was it fog, lay everywhere. The motley crew of civilians, which is what we were, that arrived at Malvern were soon awoken from our trances by the dulcet tones of the NCOs that were waiting to greet us. Without any niceties we were soon given an earful, told to *get fell in* and then bundled into the waiting TCVs. What happened after that was a bit of a blur? That we were hounded from pillar to post was no exaggeration. There was no time to take in anything; or as we were about to learn in army parlance - 'no time to take in sweet f**k all'. As David Fowler wrote in *National Service - Elvis and Me*; *if you couldn't fit three swear words into a five word sentence you weren't fit to be in the army.* And it seemed that most of them started with 'f' or 'b'. F*****g or bloody seemed to cover a multitude of grammatical expressions depending on the nuances of the emitted phrase. One very soon learned that 'f**k me!' was not an invitation to commit a carnal act with the corporal. F***, as we soon discovered, was a grammarian's delight; it could be used as a noun, adjective or verb, and no doubt in other contexts as yet undiscovered. Writing home some many days later, I recorded that *the first day was absolutely terrible - beyond belief.* Each day we were normally woken sometime just before 5.00 a.m. with the banging of dustbin lids and other metal implements, things that had clearly been designed - not for their obvious purpose in life, but as an implement to generate the maximum amount of decibels with the minimum of effort by the perpetrator. Into the bargain, it was damned well freezing cold each morning. There was no artificial heat in the 'spiders' at this time of the day.

From then we showered, shaved and dressed and were out on 'breakfast parade' in very short order. Malvern must be a very depressing place indeed we recruits thought. Each morning the hills were covered in thick fog or mist and a damp chilling atmosphere hung around the camp as we were marched - left hand behind our backs clutching our 'eating irons'. These were implements that, in civilian life, we had previously known as knife, fork and spoon. In addition to the knife, fork and spoon a tin mug was provided. The first two or three days were spent collecting our kit; boots, battledress, denims, some webbing, and other sundry items. Then boot polish had to be purchased, along with Blanco and the other necessities required for 'bulling' our kit. Her Majesty's government had not deemed it necessary for these items to be provided by our hosts. Then battle dresses and denims had to be measured and tailored to achieve for what might pass as a reasonable fit. Boots were the exception; they were tried and tested to ensure that you had a pair - actually two pairs - that were a comfortable fit. One pair was for dress wear and the other for work. Then there were the haircuts; no amount of your previous civilian tonsuring was deemed adequate to give the desired trim that these beloved NCOs demanded - you may as well have saved yourself the money you had spent. Depressingly, we had to send all our civilian clothes home; clearly, we were severing all bonds with our other life.

Along with the kitting out we were subjected to the usual administration requirements, and in Her Majesty's army this was no small task. Everything from height, weight, colour of eyes and educational attainments etc. etc. were taken and recorded. Following on was the first set of inoculations swiftly, and a little crudely administered, with barely time to say Ouch! Then the real fun began. From 5.00 a.m. onwards each day we were subjected to marching, drill parades, being taught how to 'bull' kit, and fast kit changes. These kit changes were never fast enough, thus resulting in more drill. Clearly, we were an uncoordinated lot that drove the NCOs to near despair. Naturally, such inadequacy could not go unchecked - so the result was more disciplinary parades and drill. 'Doubling', or running around the parade ground or square carrying some very heavy bit of kit above your head was a favourite punishment. Failure to carry out this task to the NCOs satisfaction resulted in ever more punishments, and so it went on until 'lights out'.

'Lights out' at 10.15 p.m., or was it 10.30 p.m., was a welcome relief. But unfortunately it didn't stop there. We were now in our own time, the period in which we now had to 'bull' all our kit to the NCOs standards. Standards, which no matter what you had achieved, grew ever more demanding. For starters, the boots that we had been issued with were new and adorned with the dimples that accompany new, heavy-duty leather. The toecaps of these boots had to be burnished to a gleaming dome of black polish. So we were soon displaying our newly acquired skill of heating the back of one of our 'eating irons' - our only spoon, which was a desert spoon - in the flame of a candle (purchased with our own money). This heated spoon then had to be ironed over the toecaps of our boots with some force to acquire a smooth finish. This was a tiresome task, which took a considerable amount of time and skill to acquire a satisfactory standard. Then, once an adequately smooth surface had been achieved one had to apply small amounts of polish, in a circulatory fashion, followed by small amounts of spit to generate an even smother and altogether more glossy finish - something that needed many hours of patient application. Brasses then had to be polished to impart a gleam well beyond the maker's original intention. These NCOs were a demanding lot. By about 2.00 a.m. in the morning one could usually grab a quick few minutes to read a letter from home, or pen a quick scrawl home - assuming you had the energy. Then it was time to crawl into your 'pit'.

At 5.00 a.m. sharp it all kicked off again. At the time I wondered how these NCOs could appear immaculately turned out and looking so fresh at this ungodly hour, and day after day. It was only much later that I realised that tiredness had obscured me to the fact that the NCOs were taking it in shifts to do the morning and evening duties.

We were tasked to be at 1TRRE for two weeks whilst they sorted us out into potential groupings ready to be sent onto the next training camp, one that the army deemed most appropriate to our perceived capabilities. Then there was the PT, more often than not it rained during these sessions on the parade ground. Why, oh why, could we not do PT in the gym when it was raining? Apparently it seemed, Sod's Law dictated that we could only use the gym on dry days. PT in wet clothes and plimsolls was not the most comfortable experience; particularly when the plimsolls were never dry for the next session. Towards the end of this two-week period, as we awaited our first posting, we suddenly found that we were starting to look, if not act, like soldiers. Two days from the end of our time at 1TRRE we had our 'Passing Off Parade', which was taken by the camp commander - someone whom we had only seen once when we were first inducted into the regiment. Naturally, this was an occasion when the NCOs harried us from 'pillar to post' to get our kit brought up to a satisfactory standard and our parade ground skills to something they deemed acceptable. Sleep was in very short supply over this period. Amazingly, the camp commander said afterwards that our parade had been of a particularly high standard. Wow! Perhaps these corporals were magicians in disguise. That the parade was over did not mean the end of it - it was merely a brief interlude before duties returned to normal.

It was only after the 'Passing off Parade' that we were told where our next posting would be. There were three destinations in the offing. The first was 6TRRE stationed at Deville Barracks at Cove near Farnborough, Hampshire. Then there was 9TRRE stationed at Morval Barracks, again near Cove. Both barracks were adjacent to each other and collectively were known as Southwood Camp. And lastly, there was 3TRRE stationed at Guillemont barracks. Again this barracks was near Cove but about one mile or so distant from Southwood Camp. It was at this time that the corporals informed us of the selections that the army had made in, according to them, its infinite wisdom. Only time would tell if the selections were really wise.

6TRRE was the camp that mainly took sappers, and a few recruits that were deemed might make NCO grade and a few that might be potential officers. 9TRRE was where sappers, potential NCOs and some potential officers were posted, and 3TRRE was the camp that took most potential officers, potential NCOs and sappers. Of course, we were all extremely curious to know where we were going next. As I recollect, it took a long time to get through the various lists and it was only after some considerable suspense that I learnt that I was to be sent to 3TRRE. Naturally, everyone wanted to know what their new camp was going to be like and the NCOs were quizzed relentlessly about what we might expect at the various destinations. We were now at the end of our two-week stint at 1TRRE and so the corporals opened up and became more relaxed about informing us about the further pleasures that we were about to enjoy. 6TRRE it seemed, was not a delight by any standards and anyone posted there could expect little enjoyment - be prepared. Those with 6TRRE on the horizon could read between the lines - it was going to be no picnic. 9TRRE was then described with a lot of hearty sarcastic laughter. It was going to be "rather like hell" the intended recipients were told. Hmm, glad I not going there thought I. And what about 3TRRE? A brief pause; *you f*****s will wish you had never been bloody well born. Hell will be like heaven compared to No. 3* we were solemnly informed. *Oh s**t!* The last two weeks had been hell enough, it surely can't get any worse, or so I thought.

After the 'Pass off Parade' we were allowed out of the camp for a few hours to visit the delights of Malvern, which was a few miles distant from our camp. The sun was shining; the town of Malvern looked lovely and quaint; suddenly, Merebrook Camp seemed not such a bad place after all if one took into account the prospect that lay ahead of us.

3TRRE, Guillemont Barracks, Cove, Hampshire

The next day, Thursday 24 October 1957, we were back to reality. Reveille was at 3.30 a.m. and we were back to the cacophony of the full complement of NCOs getting their charges ready for the transportation to their various destinations. All kit had to be packed to the regulatory standards, and our boots had to be immaculate. As for our battle dresses, the thick serge had to be ironed and creased to ridiculous degrees of sharpness. Our corporals were certainly not going to allow us to disgrace them in front of the officers and NCOs from the other regiments that were coming to collect us. It was all a bit of a hazy mad dash blur getting everything sorted out and ready for the new team that was about to collect us. At a still ridiculously early hour we were transported to Malvern Station and there acquainted with our new superiors; one second lieutenant, one sergeant and a few corporals. We had barely seen a sergeant before never mind a second lieutenant. What were they going to be like compared to our previous superiors? We did not have long wait before we found out. It rapidly became apparent that this new lot of NCOs were going to establish their authority early and beyond any question of doubt. We were rapidly entrained onto the special train that the army had requisitioned for this purpose, and soon we were all heading south with a great deal of trepidation; heading to the heartland of the British Army - the Aldershot Garrison Area. The camps of 3, 6 and 9TRRE were all situated very close to each other, and so one train was suitable for the transportation of all the recruits. At Birmingham we had to change trains for another army special to take us to Farnborough. The noise from the steam trains at Birmingham was no match for the commands emanating from the NCOs that were our new lords and masters. The sergeant quickly interpreted the silent nods and gestures from the second lieutenant, and his instructions were eagerly enacted upon by the other NCOs. One could only admire the strength of the vocal chords that could generate such decibels. The local citizenry were seen to give our lot a very wide berth indeed lest they be press-ganged as well. I think we changed stations at Birmingham as well as trains, but on that matter my memory is vague.

The journey south was mostly enjoyed in silence. The relief of not being subjected to the usual abuse was one reason, but the principal factor was undoubtedly because everyone was exceedingly worried and apprehensive about what lay ahead. The omens were already looking very bleak indeed.

Eventually we alighted from the train at Farnborough North Camp, which was the nearest station to Farnborough, and there shepherded onto the waiting TCVs to take us to our respective regiments at Deville, Morval and Guillemont Barracks.

No. 3TRRE where I was posted was an emergency camp built for units of the Canadian Army during WWII and was still doing sterling service seventeen years later. The camp comprised wooden barrack rooms of clapboard type construction, situated around a very large parade ground. Each of the barrack room complexes, known as 'spiders' could accommodate around 100-120 sappers. The 'spiders' were so called because in plan the shape of the complex resembled the shape of a spider. Each 'spider' had six legs for sleeping accommodation together with a central core block that combined toilets, showers, areas for washing kit, small troop office, small store and a large drying room. No sapper who served at No.3TRRE will ever forget the drying rooms. The official function of the drying room was obviously to dry clothes and kit - something it did exceedingly well. It has to be recognised that all the recruits, NCOs and officers were out in all weathers and the training, together with the normal infantry training, encompassed bridging and watermanship which often necessitated being waist deep in water for considerable periods of time. You were unlucky if this stint of training was carried out over any of the winter months. Guess what! The result of this was that sodden battle dresses, and more often denims, had to be dried in double quick time overnight to be ready for wear the next day. The material from which this clothing had been made had the water absorption properties of which a blotting paper manufacturer would have been proud. Consequently, these drying rooms were heated to super-hot temperatures 24 hours every day. However, the unofficial use for these drying rooms served another altogether more nefarious purpose. Here it was that the many punishment parades were carried out; but more of that later. A plan of Guillemont Barracks & Surrounding Area, circa 1957-1959, is shown in the

APPENDICES, together with my recollection of what the layout of a spider looked like.

After unceremoniously alighting from the TCVs we were soon back to the harsh realities - *get f*****g fell in; move your f*****g selves,* and so it went on. There was absolutely no time to think, every thing was done at the double, or quicker. If you were lucky you reacted quickly and correctly - if you were slow, or hesitant, heaven help you. We were soon learning that the conditions at Guillemont Barracks were turning out to be just as the NCOs at our previous camp had predicted. It very quickly became apparent that the previous standards that we had achieved at Merebrook Camp were nowhere near good enough for the NCOs and officers at Guillemont Barracks. What was it going to take to satisfy these guys? We would soon find out.

We thought we had had it hard at No. 1TRRE, well we did, but No. 3TRRE was on a different planet altogether. My first letter home written at the end of October 1957 gives a flavour of what we were about to experience:

Well, this camp has turned out to be all that it was supposed to be. Seemingly, of all the Royal Engineer Regiments this is the strictest and because of that it always turns out the best 'pass off' parade. For every intake they make you work very hard to ensure that they maintain the same high standard. In fact 3 hours after we arrived here we had to 'bull up' the room for an inspection. This meant climbing up into the roof trusses and dusting them and also getting down on the floor and polishing it with boot brushes. We also have clean new buckets which we lay out for inspection - we are not allowed to use them and must keep Brassoing them every day. Likewise, all brush handles and table tops have to be scraped with razor blades to keep them spotless. Also, all curtain rails and radiator valves must be Brassoed. All this must be done before 7.15 a.m. together with having had your breakfast. This means we are up before 5.00 a.m. every morning, and if the room doesn't please the corporal then we have to do it all again every evening for a 7.30 p.m. inspection: and we also have one every night at 9.00 p.m. irrespective of whether we have had one at 7.30 p.m.. This week we also got issued with all of our top kit i.e. packs, ammunition pouches etc. and in all we have 72 brasses to polish together with having to scrub all the webbing, and then Blanco it. Naturally, all of this has to be done in our own time and not in official working hours. Coo, what a life.

My other letters show that the working day was 5.00 a.m. till 10.30 p.m. with no respite in between and we were now working at a much higher tempo than ever before. Each room within the spiders slept, on average, 19-20 sappers, and at the entrance to each room was a little cubicle, which was reserved for the lance corporal in charge of the troop within each room. These 'Lance Jacks' as these very junior corporals were irrelevantly known, were responsible for the standards within their small domains, from sapper turn-out to room cleanliness. Their reputation hung on the standard of their troop, and by hook or by crook they weren't going to let a new bunch of national servicemen spoil that reputation.

One spider contained six rooms or troops, with a maximum total of 120 sappers within each spider. These six troops were collectively known as a Party. A second lieutenant was responsible for these six troops, together with a sergeant, perhaps two or three full corporals, and six lance corporals. The number of sappers within each intake could vary depending upon the time of year. Towards the end of any year the number of university graduates would increase after finals in May/June, whereas the number of others could vary depending upon extraneous circumstances. The normal minimum intake was usually in the region of 70-90 sappers.

Because the 'Lance Jack's' reputation depended on his troop's achievements it was clear that nothing was going to impair that reputation, and he made it known in no uncertain terms that *you f*****s are not going to let me down.* And so the daily grind of bulling room and kit started. Everything that moved was cleaned and polished and cleaned again. Everything that was stationary was cleaned and polished and dusted, and dusted again. The wooden floors were polished until they gleamed and then you daren't walk on them in you boots. 'Bumpers', as I recall, was the name given to the heavy floor mops that were used to impart the gleam after an application of polish. This was heavy work. But such was the cussedness of some of these NCOs that they felt that only by getting down on your hands and knees, with a shoe brush in hand, could the best finish be achieved. This was every bit as hard work as the 'bumpers' and a lot slower. Thereafter, bits of carpet or heavy duty felt were laid down to enable you to move around without too much disturbance to the gleam that had been imparted to these floors. I remember not where we got these bits of rudimentary protection, but I guess that earlier troops before us had bequeathed these objects for our benefit. Then there was the dusting - everything had to be dusted from the exposed rafters in the roof space of the single storey room to the drawer slides on the small chest of wooden drawers, i.e. if you were fortunate enough to have a small chest of drawers. It did not matter how often these slides were dusted the wooden slides collected a new deposit of micro grains of wood dust immediately they were re-opened. This gave the lance corporal rich pickings if he had it in for you. One opening of the drawer by the corporal - usually clumsily - could guarantee a deposit of wood dust. It did not matter how slight a deposit - *you f*****g untidy bastard.* At this juncture it would have been more than fatal to correct him about your legitimate parentage. And we hadn't even got around to our kit at this stage. The reason for this was that in these first few days at No. 3TRRE our battle-dresses and denims were again checked over for a proper fit, and if necessary, adjusted very quickly by the civilian tailor that served the camp. After these initial few days we were then let loose on our kit. More Blanco, boot polish, dusters and sundry other bits and pieces were purchased from the NAAFI (Navy, Army, Air Force Institutes) all out of our meagre 28/- per week wage. It did not leave much to be spent on 'choc' bars and other goodies to top up hungry appetites. My abiding memory of the NAAFI at this time was Paul Anka singing *Diana*, which was in the top spot of the Hit Parade during October 1957. It was being relayed relentlessly during that period and at a volume that was, unbelievably, greater than the decibels our NCOs could muster. Unfortunately, it did generate a great feeling for missed loved ones, and a degree of homesickness. After Paul Anka, Elvis soon attained top spot, and the volume of sound never relented - but it was still a welcome relief from the raucous tones of our NCOs.

Soon after the initial inductions, which again included the dreaded haircut, we were then issued with our rifles - Lee Enfield .303 rifles. It was soon instilled into us that no matter what, that rifle must be under your control at all times, otherwise it had to be kept in a locked steel cabinet beside your bed, and of course, the bolt of your rifle had to be stored separately, again secreted in a locked cabinet. Anyone who lost bolt or rifle, or both, could expect to spend the next two years at Her Majesty's pleasure in the military prison at Colchester or, if it the offence was deemed sufficiently serious, in the other even less salubrious establishment at Shepton Mallet. Neither establishment fostered an existence to be entertained by anyone in full control of their faculties.

But the rifles were not for show; soon we were on the parade ground under the watchful eye of the sergeant and corporals and occasionally the officer in charge of the party. The drilling was relentless and nothing was ever good enough for our masters. Anything not up to scratch was done over and over again ad infinitum, until a small degree of satisfaction was obtained. But there were always one or two persons that unfortunately could not tell their left foot from their right foot, or more accurately, could not co-ordinate their feet and arms in the normal fashion. This small group was known as 'the awkward squad'. When marching, instead of swinging their right arm back as their left foot stepped forward, they could only move them in a contra fashion, i.e. the left hand went forward at the same time as their left foot. This was unfortunate for these few individuals. Such an action on the parade ground was guaranteed to send any NCO within eyeshot totally ballistic. *You f*****g uncoordinated wanker. You stupid f****r. Get a f*****g grip sapper*; all shouted into your ear at very close range. And so it went on… Anyone subjected to such obscenities, for whatever reason, had to keep control of their emotions and not let it get you down. Just focus and get on with it was the best you could do. To do otherwise would ultimately lead to despair and worse. Some did break under the pressure. Naturally, the obscenities were the least of your troubles. If you did not focus and get a grip, then a punishment parade was in the offing.

This is where we return to those super-heated drying rooms with their open raftered roofs and concrete floors. Everyone was subjected to a punishment parade for whatever reason - it was part of the training. The only thing you could do was to give your best effort on every task and try to keep the punishments to the minimum. These punishments were always given after 6.00 p.m. in the evening, in the period that was euphemistically called your 'free time'- some hopes! At these punishment parades you had to report to the senior corporal in charge in the drying room at the appointed time. Dress was best battledress and best boots - all gleaming and highly polished, together with greatcoat, and kitted out in full battle order, including steel helmet and rifle. The greatcoat was a most decided encumbrance in the heat and humidity of these super-heated drying rooms. All kit was inspected and anything less than a very high standard meant another punishment parade, and that was before you had even started the evening. Our rifles, as well as having to be clean externally, also had to be spotless internally. Bolts were removed, polished, and oiled, and the internal rifling of the barrel of the gun had to be gleaming. This was done by pulling a weighted cord attached to a small piece of oiled rag through the barrel of the rifle until the innards were gleaming. A 'pull through' was the name given to this most unspectacular, but necessary, little bit of kit. Even the steel studs on the soles of our boots had to be polished to a bright steely shine with absolutely no modicum of rust to be seen. *Solvol Autosol*, as I remember it, was the chrome cleaner that could be purchased from Halfords, at great expense, to impart an outstanding gleam to all steel surfaces, e.g. boot studs, bayonet, jack knife, rifle bolt etc. I seem to recall that it also worked well on our brasses. If you got through this very rigorous inspection then at least you could commence the punishment with a degree of hope.

Then it would start. One hour of solid drilling, all in double quick time, by a squad of seemingly sadistic NCOs taking it in turn to grind you down. In the heat of this hothouse this was nothing short of torture by another name. Often, the last fifteen minutes of these punishment parades would be marking time - again in double quick time. By the time the hour was up you were barely able to co-ordinate your legs - they were as jelly. But any relaxation now was fatal and another punishment would be meted out - you just had to grit your teeth and get through it somehow. It was better to faint in the heat, and some did, than be seen to give less than 100%. If you survived without further retribution you then had the task of being able to look forward to another repair job on your beloved kit. Such parades always took their toll on your best boots and BD. These repair jobs were something that had to be attended to in double quick time - and in your own time. The fear always was that if you got another punishment parade before you had time to 'bull up' your kit again you were well on the way to more parades - ad infinitum. The free time was a joke.

Then there were the kit changes. These were another of the sadistic pleasures that our NCOs liked to inflict on their charges. Without warning, you would be instructed to change into your best BD, boots, and Battle Order webbing for an inspection outside the spider. No sooner had you got on parade and been given the quick 'once over' then the order would be given to get changed again and *get fell in for PT*. Into the barrack room in double quick time, best kit stored away, and out again in PT kit. Another quick once over and then *get changed into working denims and get fell in outside*. And then another fast change of kit, and once more outside in your best BD etc. etc. This seemed to go on interminably at a faster and faster pace to please our masters. Heaven help you if you paraded outside with some bit of kit missing or in a poor state; you could be sure the drying room beckoned.

Our free time was when you 'bulled' up all your kit or carried out room cleaning duties ready for the morning inspections. Our ever-officious lance corporals were extremely conscientious when it came to inspections. Each week one sapper was made Room Senior and it was his duty to mobilise the other room members to put in their best efforts to get the room to the required standard for the daily inspections. On Saturdays and Sundays there were no inspections, and on Sundays, unless there was a special event on, one could lie in bed all day if you so wished. Sadly, there was never enough time available for this luxury and a long lie in was normally till 7.30 a.m. or thereabouts. And in between duties there was the obligatory letter, or letters, to be written to parents or loved ones. The receipt of letters from loved ones at home was always something that meant a lot to the national serviceman. What was not enjoyed was the receipt of a 'Dear John', which many did receive. For some this was shrugged off as just one of those things - even although it was apparent that some hurt had been dealt. For others it was a bit of a body blow that took time to get over. As might be expected, this usually had negative effects on the sapper's performance until he got over the event. But 'Dear Johns' or not, the army marched on - just *get over it princess* was the army's advice. *Roll on death - demobs too far away* was the light-hearted call of many.

Within each room one could expect to encounter many characters. One of these in our room was Alexander M, or 'Zander' as he was known. 'Zander' was stockily built, very strong and hard as nails. 'Zander' was from Macduff in the north east of Scotland and had spent his years prior to being conscripted on the fishing boats in the North Sea, and having to graft extremely hard during the time at sea. He was a lovely lad, always smiling and ever willing to help, but he had one big drawback - he was from the north east of Scotland and his accent was as broad as the sea itself. No one understood him. Consequently, as the only other Scot in the room I had to act as his interpreter, and even I struggled with his accent. How he coped after he passed off from No. 3TRRE I don't know. It was not easy for 'Zander', but it didn't seem to get him down, he soldiered on so to speak.

Time was now late October early November and drill parades were an ever present in our working day. For as much time as I spent on the parade ground as a sapper and later as an officer I could not recall whether it was a tarmac or concrete parade ground; I had to rely on Ian Chappell to remind me that it was a tarmacadam parade ground. *Am I hurting you sapper* was a rhetorical question often asked by the party sergeant. *No sergeant, you would reply. Well I bloody well ought to be; I'm standing on your hair.* Duly translated, this meant get a haircut before the next parade. It was futile, even dangerous, to indicate that you had had one only a few days previously.

By now our kit was starting to gleam ever more brightly and the creases in our battledresses had never been sharper. The trick regarding your battle dress trousers was to turn them inside out and to shave along the lines where sharp crease were meant to be to reduce the thickness of the serge material. Then, turn the BD back the correct way and then iron it to provide a reasonably sharp crease in absolutely the correct location. Then again, turn the trousers inside out and soap the inside of the crease line with a bar of damp soap sufficient to leave a very slight deposit of soap on the crease, but not too much soap - that could be disastrous. Then turn the trousers back again and iron them, again, along the crease line to give a super-sharp crease that would stay in place for a good length of time with only the minimum of maintenance. Too much soap applied to the inside of the trousers soon showed up in wet weather, when small bubbles and soapy deposits would appear on the outside of the trousers. Never ever let that happen on parade lest the 'Wrath of Cain' would descend upon you. Chains were another ruse that the long service men employed to get a decent turn down at the bottom of the trouser legs and so let the trouser hang properly over the gaiters. Normally they only adopted this trick when on parade. This subterfuge meant the deployment of a light chain placed on the inside of the trouser leg at the bottom where the turn down occurred. At No. 3TRRE this tactic was officially frowned upon, but it was fairly obvious that, on occasions, a 'Nelsonian' eye was deployed, depending upon the seniority of the serviceman involved.

The one parade that no one objected to was the church parade. I cannot recollect how often we had these parades, but I think it was between one and two per fortnight. Everyone had to attend church parade, which meant all the sappers of all denominations within a given Party would be lined up and marched to the small chapel, which we had within the precincts of the camp. Once at the chapel everyone was 'fallen out' and those that wished to go into the chapel could do so, if not, you were then allowed to do your own thing for the duration of the service, which was usually just under one hour long. The chapel was also open during non-service hours for anyone who wished to enter for prayer or meditation. Many a sapper, religious or otherwise, took advantage of any brief respite in duties to avail themselves of a little quiet time away from the hurly burly of army life. The other parade of note was the mealtime parade, which was usually reserved for new recruits within the first three or four weeks of arriving at 3TRRE. Each mealtime the troop would *get fell in* and then marched to the cookhouse with eating irons, plus tin mug, held in your left hand, and behind your back. The other arm had to be swung briskly in time to the marching rhythm. This small task was often the downfall of the 'awkward squad' that could not master the simultaneous rhythm of left foot forward left arm back. Once in the cookhouse the troop would be lined up for service from one of the many cooks behind the service counter. Food was dished out rather unceremoniously and it never looked particularly appetising. Many, if not most, complained about the quality of the food, but I cannot say that I ever found it terribly bad - perhaps not great, but not bad. Maybe it was because I had only been used to standard fare that I did not feel aggrieved about the quality on offer. However, it would appear from some of my letters home that we did not seem to be getting enough to eat and *please send food parcel* was a not uncommon request. The standard issue tin mug that we were given had one great benefit - it could not be easily broken, or otherwise made useless. Unfortunately, it had one major disadvantage. If any hot liquid was put into the tin mug then scalded lips and mouth were a distinct possibility. Best left until the contents were cold, but then that was not a particularly appetising thought after the completion of a night exercise during the cold winter months - you couldn't win.

On completion of the meal you then made your own way back to the 'spider', but only after you had completed one task - that of cleaning your 'eating irons'. A relatively straightforward task you might think. It was, but it brought with it elements of danger. Immediately outside the exit from the cookhouse was a galvanised metal tank, which was full of boiling water, and constantly being topped up by injections of very hot steaming water. The eating implements had to be scrupulously cleaned in this tank of near lethal boiling water. Many a sapper had the burns to show for it, and this was not an operation that could be avoided. More times than not when exiting the cookhouse you would find that a 'Lance Jack' would be stationed close by the hot water tank and if he thought anyone had scrimped their cleansing duties then a rigorous inspection of the eating irons ensued. Heaven forbid if the remains of your meal was to be found on any of your implements. If the corporal was from your own party or squadron, then it was usually the drying room for you. If the NCO was from another squadron then all sorts of punishments could be heaped upon you. 'Jankers', the army slang for confinement to camp was never considered a suitable slap on the wrists. We were all confined to camp anyway during our first eight weeks of training, so 'Jankers' would have had no effect whatsoever. In all probability you would be recalled, after hours, to the parade ground in your best BD, boots and battle order webbing and made to 'double' around the very large parade ground carrying a Bren gun or other heavy bit of kit above your head. More than thrice around the ground was just about the best that could be managed before collapse started to set in. Anything less, and the corporal in attendance would inflict some further retribution. These punishments were bad enough, but since they were done in your free time then that was a restriction on the time you had available to 'bull' your kit, the room or whatever other tasks you had to complete that evening; and failure to complete these other tasks merely gave rise to ever more punishment. Lights out at 10.30 p.m. merely meant the candles coming on and staying on until the 'wee sma hours'. 2.00 a.m. was quite normal for a realistic 'lights out'. And of course lighting candles was verboten within the sleeping accommodation, consequently all these tasks that were carried out by candlelight were done within the toilets or drying room. We certainly saw more than enough of that damned drying room. It did however have one big plus - it was warm - well actually too warm, tropically warm. At times this was much appreciated because our sleeping accommodation of 19-20 bodies only had a small potboiler stove at the far end of the room to heat the space. In the summer months this was not a problem; unfortunately during the winter months of October, November, December and January when I was there it was a considerable problem. The heat was to all intents and purposes non-existent. For what it was worth we had to take it in turns to stoke the little potboiler with the fuel provided to generate heat as best possible. However, since we spent all the day between reveille and 5.00 p.m. or 6.00 p.m. outside in the training areas - usually getting wet, and certainly getting cold, then no one was at home, so to speak, to stoke our modest source of heat. This could only be done when we returned to the barrack room with the result that it was only at 'lights out' that any heat started to emanate from the stove, by which time stoking had to cease. The air was often quite blue, even very blue, from the comments of my fellow roommates. F**k, b*****d and c**t were frequently to be heard.

One thing the sappers were particularly fastidious about was personal hygiene. Going on parade with highly polished boots was fine, but dirt under finger nails or elsewhere was strictly taboo - something that the Guards Battalions did not appear to be so strict about - although I'm sure they would deny this. Foot inspections were abundant and a liberal amount of foot powder was made available for our use. NCOs would parade the showers area to ensure that, where possible, everyone was making a proper effort to keep clean. *Pull back your foreskin and shower it clean* or other more fruity expressions were hollered out by these enthusiastic 'chappies'; *we'll be carrying out an inspection to see that you've done it properly.* Fortunately, as far as I can remember, we were spared that indignity. It was just a threat to make sure that we had made an effort. And of course each room within the 'spider' had a bath book, which each sapper had to fill in to record his bathing habits. This was something the lance corporal in charge of the room checked regularly to ensure that everyone had been having frequent baths. I retrieved this bit of information from one of my letters home to Lorna but my memory does not record us ever having the time for such a luxury - at least, not in the early days of training. One thing that did make hygiene difficult was the fact that all the sinks were minus the sink plugs. Most sappers, as far as I can remember, wrote home for a 'one and a quarter inch sink plug' to be sent ASAP - something that was guarded zealously for the rest of their service. Many were the camps that could be found to be deficient of this small but necessary bit of equipment.

One of our first night exercises was for small groups of us sappers to attempt to recapture a lit lantern from a group of NCOs. The lantern was positioned about three quarters of a mile distant from our start point and the approaches were patrolled and guarded by numerous NCOs. If you were spotted, then you were out of the exercise. Naturally, it had been raining quite heavily during the day and early evening, and, as we had at times to crawl for several hundred yards or so through thick scrub, we got thoroughly sodden. At the end of the exercise in the early hours we then had to run back about 2-3 miles, in by now heavy rain, to get back to camp. These drying rooms were never more welcoming

By the end of week four we had been in training for six weeks - two at Merebrook Camp and four at Guillemont Barracks. By now we were starting to look and act like soldiers. Apart from the incessant drilling on the parade ground there was the gas mask training. As a matter of course everyone had been kitted out with the old type gas masks, which had been left over kit from WWII. To say that they were cumbersome to wear was an understatement. After having been shown how to assemble and wear them correctly, and how to control your breathing when wearing them, then came the exercises using them. At this point it should be said that on the perimeter of the camp there were one or two old brick built air raid shelters - another hangover from WWII. These shelters were single storey in height with flat slab concrete roofs. The shelters themselves were of a considerable length and comprised a great many empty rooms which had no doors, but each of the door openings were staggered in their location such that no blast could sweep through the shelter without being impeded in its travel. Very similar in fact, to how a traditional dark room would have been laid out. Consequently, no natural light penetrated these constructions further than the first room within the shelter and there was no artificial light within these shelters. So it was that after being kitted out in full gas mask order you would then be shepherded in small groups to the entrance of the shelters. Once assembled the NCOs would then throw in a number of smoke bombs into the shelters, and as soon as that happened then the small groups of sappers were harangued and shouted at to run as fast as possible through the maze of rooms and exit from the far entrance in the shortest period of time. Breathing in the gas masks was difficult at the best of times. Visibility was abysmal at any time and with the combination of smoke, no light, condensation within the mask and NCOs hurling abuse at you to speed up, the whole experience sometimes became quite traumatic. Many a sapper would be near to fainting; and disorientation was a constant problem. Adding to the various difficulties was the fact that panic was never far away. And with dense smoke pulsating through the shelters pulling off the gas mask was not an option. We were always very glad when these sessions were over.

It was around this time that our party of six troops - approximately 100 sappers - was put on administration duties for between 10 - 14 days. This was a duty that each of the training parties in the regiment had to undertake during their 14 week basic training period. In effect, this meant attending to all the menial, and other tasks, that kept our regiment of 900 or more soldiers functioning. The Party Officer responded to calls from the headquarters squadron, aka, ('C' Squadron), to provide bodies for whatever duty was needed at any particular time. Guard duties, cookhouse duties, various cleaning duties and a multitude of minor tasks to keep everyone one of us occupied. If any sapper was not occupied doing a meaningful duty then the officer or sergeant could be relied upon to devise something to keep us out of mischief. The tasks could be as varied as the day was long. I was fortunate that I rarely got any boring tasks although on occasions I wish I had. The recurring duty during this period was the old reliable one of guard duty. For this you had to parade at the appointed hour - 6.00 p.m. as I recall, - for a 24 hour spell of duty at the guardhouse. You had to be in your best BD, boots, Battle Order webbing and rifle, all highly polished, Blancoed or cleaned, ready for inspection. Heaven help you if you failed to meet the standard that the Guard Commander required. More punishments and extra duties could be expected to follow. These guard duties consisted of 2 hours on and four hours off, or 'stags', as these shifts were called. During the 'off period' you normally slept in the guardroom in your BD with rifle at your side, but minus webbing, ready to respond quickly if there was a requirement to do so. The best man on parade, selected by the Guard Commander, was called 'The Stickman' and could sometimes be excused a few tasks when on duty. At this time the IRA were active in the south of England attempting to raid army camps to acquire weapons or explosives for their own nefarious purpose. The very first raid they ever carried out was in 1955 at a REME Camp at Arborfield Barracks, which was a few miles north of 3TRRE. The raid was a partial success and they got a quantity of rifles and ammunition - largely because of the surprise that such an event could take place. Thereafter, all regiments in Southern Command were on 'Red Alert' a lot of the time when it was considered that a threat was imminent. At 3TRRE, being, arguably, the premier Training Regiment for the Royal Engineers at that particular time, 3TRRE carried the largest supply of explosives of all types in Southern Command, and a very large number of rifles, Bren guns and Sten guns etc., consequently, security was extremely tight. During these guard duties, squads of two man patrols known as 'roving pickets' would patrol around the camp at night checking all the doors to see that they were locked, and to check out all the various quiet or dark areas to ensure that nothing untoward was happening. These patrols were equipped with pick handles, or pick helves as we called them, ready to tackle any intruder.

Another admin. task was the supposedly dreaded cookhouse duty. In fact, this was not as bad as made out. Peeling potatoes was boring but bearable, although the atmosphere was always heavy and unpleasant due to the abundant condensation that hung in the air. Serving food at the counter, if the regular staff were short-handed, was equally OK but the regulars easily recognised a new recruit and you would be implored, or worse, to heap on more food than was normally allowed. I think I only every had two stints in the cookhouse - the first for peeling potatoes over an extra long shift during which time, in a quiet moment, I recollect being propositioned by a big burly cook. Whatever was he on about I wondered as I embarrassedly wriggled out of the situation. The other shift was altogether more taxing. It involved scrubbing clean the greasy cookhouse floor at the end of the day when all meals had been served - it was a decidedly greasy, grubby, and unpleasant job. And then you had to get yourself clean. My letter home at that time indicates that I had a hot bath at the end of the shift - a decided luxury.

It was, however, the other more unpleasant administration tasks that remain in the mind long after the event. Twice during this time the Provost Sergeant in charge of the Regimental Police at our camp requested assistance when he was short staffed. His domain was the regimental detention centre, otherwise know as 'The Block'; a collection of cold bare cells at the far corner of the camp surrounded by a high security fence. Here-it-was that sappers who had transgressed were imprisoned for the duration of their sentence, which I think from memory, was for a four-week maximum sentence. A longer sentence than this and the soldier would be sent to Colchester to serve his punishment, or worse still, to Shepton Mallet. 'The Block' was an exceedingly unpleasant establishment where the detainees wore only loose fitting denims and boots with no laces. Punishment was strict and harsh; you certainly did not want to end up there. This little domain was ruled over by Provost Sergeant H, a short stocky man and a Scotsman, as I seem to recall. His turnout was never less than immaculate. His battledress always seemed to be of a finer material that the rest of us had, and the creases therein were eye-wateringly sharp. He was not a man to be messed with on any occasion and commanded his domain with a rod of iron.

So it was that during this admin. period he received information that the police in Glasgow had detained a sapper from 3TRRE who had gone AWOL. As was normal on these occasions he would send one of his corporals and a sapper from his troop to collect the recalcitrant soldier. However, he was short staffed and requested that a sapper from the admin. squad be sent to assist his NCO. So, as I was not allocated to any other duty I was duly despatched to 'The Block' in best BD and boots. There the Provo Sergeant gave his NCO the appropriate instructions and armed with the appropriate travel warrants we set off early one morning for Glasgow. When we arrived at the police station where the sapper was detained we were given a complimentary sandwich and other small refreshments. On leaving the police station the NCO signed for the prisoner, and the police duly provided us with transport back to the train station for our journey south. Once we got to the station, and before leaving the police van, the NCO, to my horror, handcuffed the prisoner to me for the long journey back to camp. These were desperate men who did not want to be in the army and would make any attempt to evade custody, if at all possible. As it so happened the prisoner made no serious attempt to escape although we were subjected to the usual abuse throughout the journey, and our parentage was clearly a topic on which he felt qualified to speak with more than a little bitterness.

At Birmingham we had to change trains and at this point the miscreant decide he needed the toilet. However, the NCO was clearly wise to the fact that this was a possible ruse to make an escape attempt because of the fact that at this time the prisoner would be released from the 'cuffs'. So the NCO resisted his desperate calls and made him wait until we had boarded the second train south. Once on the train there was no escape from the train toilets - the train was moving and the windows were too small by far to afford an exit. When we reached Farnborough Station an army TCV was waiting for us, and the rest of the journey passed off without incident. Never the less, it had been a bit of an nerve-racking experience; not one that I wanted again.

But such is army life that a few days later a second request came from the Provost Sergeant - he again needed a sapper to carry out the same duty, because, as before, he was still short staffed. Sod's Law - I was again not allocated to any particular task, and since I had done this before, then I was obviously the sapper for the job. *Damn and blast these sods that kept going AWOL.* As before, I reported to 'The Block' duly kitted out in my best BD and boots. Provost Sergeant H was satisfied with my turnout, so the NCO, a different one this time, was given the appropriate travel warrants and so we set off once more. Again, we were heading for Glasgow - the Greenock area, as I seem to remember. After duly reporting to the police station we were again watered and fed and then escorted back to the train station for our journey south. This time, however, when we arrived at the station we decamped from the police van, and to my even greater horror, the NCO did not see fit to handcuff the prisoner to me. He was given a very strict warning about trying to escape, but it was left at that. Bloody hell thought I, this could get rather fraught. Suddenly, I was not sure whether it was best to have a desperado handcuffed to me, or the alternative with one who had a much better chance of 'legging it'. Nevertheless, we entrained and set off for Birmingham and the journey passed incident free. The prisoner was not abusive and in fact, seemed rather quiet, as well he might, having been caught after a few months on the run.

Hours later we arrived at Birmingham for the obligatory change of trains. Whether it was Birmingham New Street or Birmingham Snow Hill I do not remember, but I do recollect that the concourse was large and open and had what was known as a terrazzo or marble floor, which meant that it was hard, and in certain conditions, slippery. This was the time to be on the alert. We negotiated the alighting from the first train and as we were proceeding across the main concourse our man in custody made his break for freedom. He chose a moment when attentions were distracted by some distant ruckus and off he bolted making straight for one of the exits. Now, I had always prided myself on being reasonably fleet of foot, and after my six weeks, or thereby, of army training I was in good condition. Both the corporal and myself set off in hot pursuit with the sound of 'tackity' boots echoing off the hard floor - a sound that remains with me to this day. It was then that I realised, to my horror, that I was indeed quite fast on my feet. I was overtaking the prisoner at a faster rate than the NCO, and soon I was going to be upon him - on my own - at least for a short spell. *Bloody hell!*

I had never been much of a rugby player at school - I had only ever made the third fifteen; soccer had been my preferred sport. There was nothing for it but to attempt a rugby tackle from behind and hope for the best. It was with more than a little surprise that I found that I had executed what was perhaps the only perfect tackle that I had ever made and was ever likely to make. We both hit the deck with a thump, but I at least had him to somewhat cushion my landing, and I had already prepared myself for the impact. He, on the other hand, was taken slightly by surprise. All this meant that by the time he had recovered his senses the NCO had arrived on the scene and together, after only a slight altercation, the 'cuffs' were out and I had a close travelling companion for the remainder of the journey back to camp. The rest of the journey passed uneventfully and we arrived back at 'The Block' without further mishap. I did not give much for his chances during the rest of his time in detention - which he had undoubtedly lengthened by trying to make an escape bid. Of course, time in detention was not the end of it. Any time AWOL or in custody did not count as service, and so two full years still had to be served.

But there was still more fraught admin to come. Cambridge Military Hospital (named after the Duke of Cambridge) was located in Aldershot, and at that time it did not have a very good reputation. As far as I am aware it dealt with most medical and psychological conditions army personnel were likely to suffer. In, what I presume was the psychological wing, were men who were being treated for a multitude of psychological disorders. Patients who were supervised day and night by trained staff. At night, at lights out time, these patients were locked in their rooms and closely monitored to ensure that they did not commit suicide, or attempt to damage their rooms. When the hospital was short of staff our regiment provided sappers from the administration troop to help out with non-medical duties. I suspect that other regiments and battalions from the Aldershot Area did likewise. Of course, Sod's Law was to strike several times more. On more than one occasion it happened that I, along with a few others, was tasked with assisting the over-night staff at the hospital. In reality this meant that when these disturbed patients were locked in their rooms for the night one of us sappers had to be locked in with them until reveille the next day. Ostensibly, this was to stop them committing suicide if they so attempted it. However, the big worry was that these men were, in some instances, just as likely to attack the night staff as attempt suicide. This was a night duty that was extremely fraught. There was a panic button in the room to summon help if it was needed, but with few staff on duty one could not rely on instant assistance. These nights were passed with much trepidation and more than a little fear. It was always wise to sit as near the panic button as possible. Fortunately, there were no incidents during my stints at this establishment, but they were not uncommon. This was a most unpleasant duty and one that was not at all welcome. Furthermore, you still had to be prepared for some other duties when you returned back to camp in the morning, it having been assumed that you had had a peaceful night - some hopes!

And then there was Hawley Lake situated about one mile or so from the camp. It was here that the REs from our camp and the surrounding camps conducted their Bailey bridging and watermanship training. Watermanship in particular, meant having navigable water on which to sail and navigate our various rafts and crafts and on which to construct our pontoon bridges. Unfortunately, in the winter of 1957 the frosts were severe and Hawley Lake, large as it was, was frozen for long periods of time. Naturally, this was not a deterrent to the army who decreed that training must carry on. And so it was that small squads of us sappers in the admin. troop would be aroused from our slumbers somewhere between 3.30 and 4.00 a.m. to 'kit-up' and double down to the lake, there to break the ice for the training party that would be arriving later in the morning. This was not a duty that could be undertaken in a bleary haze; one had to be on full alert. The ice thickness was variable and footings were not in the least secure, particularly if you could not see where you were treading due to the falls of snow covering the ice and the ground. Many the sapper that ended up in the drink, but still the work had to be carried out. Brass monkeys it seemed were not the only primates likely to suffer from lost appendages. Then it was back to camp, hopefully in time for breakfast, a change of denims and perhaps more duties. One never knew what the next hour would bring. One thing was for sure, admin. fortnight was never boring.

Administration fortnight over, things returned to normal. This meant more 'bulling' and inspections, although this did tend to recede to a degree after awhile to be replaced by drilling on the square and welcome visits to the firing ranges. Bisley and other army firing ranges were located nearby and within easy driving distance. I have to confess I enjoyed this part of the training firing our .303 Lee Enfields over 100, 200, 400 and sometimes 800 yards. And the same with the Bren guns which were decidedly more ear shattering if a few were discharged at the same time, and they usually were. My letters to Lorna show that I got a First Class Certificate for firing the Bren guns, but of the Lee Enfield I say nothing. I assume I had not done so well in this category even although I preferred it to the Bren gun. The other weapon that we also got to use was the Sten gun, but this activity was, in the main, restricted to the short 25-50 yard ranges at the camp. We soon found out that this little weapon was of equal benefit to the enemy as it was to the user. It could go off at any time, and for Gods sake, you didn't dare drop the bloody thing otherwise live rounds could be guaranteed to be fired off in every direction, regardless of the disposition of the safety catch. It could probably have been guaranteed to hit a barn door, provided you had hold of the handle of the door. At any greater distance, then good luck to you matey! However, the most fun part of the weapon training was the time that we spent on the ranges camped out under ground sheets. Each sapper had been issued with a ground sheet as part of his normal equipment. This was a large sheet of moderately heavy waterproof material that was used as a waterproof cloak or poncho, but could also be used as a ground sheet when camping alfresco. On the camping exercises on the ranges each pair of sappers would be given an extra ground sheet for the duration of the exercise. These pairs would then share a bivouac that comprised one ground sheet laid on the ground and the other two sheets rigged up to form overhead protection for the duration of the camp. Space for sleeping was absolutely minimal and each pair had to sleep head to toe to achieve some degree of comfort. Food had to be cooked in the camp and groups were formed and allotted the requisite tasks to enable us to survive the duration of the camp, including the dreaded latrine squad. Of course this was all secondary to the prime reason for the camp, which was the training and use of the Lee Enfield rifles and Bren guns, which we were able to fire all day long. In the evening the troop officer in charge, who also slept out with the trainees, would allocate security duties, which meant very strict patrols (roving pickets) and watches all night long to guard against an IRA raid. Great care was always taken in the siting of the secure area where all the weaponry and ammunition could be kept safe overnight. I enjoyed weapon training and for me this was a fun part of my time at 3TRRE.

Interspersed with this we had the usual route marches. In the first weeks these were normally about three miles in length, but that did not last long. Soon it was the nine-mile marches in full Field Service Marching Order (FSMO) with rifles and all packs loaded, and our steel helmet slung on our backpack. These tin hats were a damned nuisance to say the least. Time, as I recollect, was two hours, so it was more a fast jog than a march. This was very hard on some recruits who were not up to the physical standard required to achieve this pace. Naturally, the corporals did this in PT kit, so they were able to double back and forth, up and down the line, shouting and encouraging the party, particularly those that were less able. The party always worked as a team, so the corporals would take webbing and other bits of kit off the less able sappers and transfer that extra load amongst the others to ensure that the whole troop could complete the march [sic] in the allotted time. No one ever complained about this redistribution of load. One day you might just need some assistance yourself and you had to be able to rely on your other troop members to help you out.

Somewhere around the midpoint of our time at 3TRRE we were given an inoculation, which consisted of three injections or potions in one jab. What they were for I remember not, but this was a time when the army permitted you to be excused duties for 36 hours. For some, the injections had no visible effects. For others it was a time of a good deal of discomfort, and for others it was a most decidedly unpleasant period, although recovery was swift. I was lucky enough to fall into the middle category, so I was not too upset, but it still meant a grotty few hours and some time spent in bed to recover from the injection.

Somewhere during this mid-point in training we were shown the mandatory films on venereal disease and smoking, and what horrors could be inflicted upon you should you partake of these pleasures! I also remember seeing diseased lungs in a jar, presumably immersed in a formaldehyde solution. I had never smoked before entering the army, and after seeing the samples of blackened and withered lungs I was certainly not going to do so in the future. Sadly however, some did not seem to care, and continued with the nicotine habit. The army had at least tried its best...

The first few weeks of our training had concentrated on infantry duties but as we entered the second half of our twelve week spell at No. 3TRRE we became more immersed in specialist engineering training (field engineering) as well as continuing with the infantry training. This training was of considerably more interest. First up, we had a week or so of digging trenches, observation posts, and building revetments for these various bits of ground level protection. And then there was the laying of barbed wire encampments. This latter exercise necessitated the wearing of very stout protective gloves because the wire was exceptionally sharp. The coils of barbed wire were, as I seem to recollect, known as Dannert Coils. At the conclusion of this short period we had exercise *Hedgehog* to complete this part of our training. This was an exercise that extended over a period of 36-48 hours depending on our acquired skills and the speed with which we could execute these skills. In other words, how fast and how long could we dig for? Trenches were dug and the sides revetted and then a blast shelter had similarly to be dug and revetted. The whole encampment then had to be protected by barbwire or Dannert Coil fences. In the part of the training area we had been allocated for this exercise the soil was hard clay. Digging was damned hard work. Naturally, Sod had decreed that the weather should be inclement - to put it mildly. Only a few hours into the exercise and we were 'somping' wet and at the completion we were carrying a double weight of clothing due to the sodden mass that was our denims. During this exercise I had removed my helmet because of the discomfort of wearing it. Unfortunately, I had left it upside down with the consequent effect after a particularly heavy rainstorm. When I was instructed to wear it again it was decidedly uncomfortable. The drying rooms were never more welcoming than at the end of these types of exercise.

Interspersed with the training we had the usual emergency fire drills except that things were always so hectic that we could never make out if it had been a true emergency or merely an exercise. Following on from this we had a week or more spent doing mine-warfare. This consisted of seeing and recognising the various types of mines, from anti-tank mines to anti-personnel mines. Then we had to learn how to lay these mines hidden from view, and for maximum destructive effect. But worse was to follow - how to find these mines when laid, and then lift them again without subsequent harm. This could be done during daylight hours with a very watchful eye and a great deal of care as we angled our slim steel rod of a bayonet into the soil to locate the anti-tank mines. Or, in the case of anti-personnel mines, you had to gently sweep your hand over the ground ready to detect the slim protruding antennae of the hidden device that could trigger an explosion. All of these detection techniques were carried out from the prone, or crawling position on your stomach on the ground; you were very close indeed to these buried horrors. After locating them the devices had to be lifted without disturbance to the triggering mechanism. Live explosive was not used, but buried thunder flashes took the place of the explosive material. Two flashes were used for an anti-personnel mine, and a batch of six flashes for an anti-tank mine. The anti-tank mines took the form of a concrete pancake about 12-14" in diameter and around 4" thick. They were shaped in the form of a real mine with a slightly bevelled top surface. The six-pack of thunder flashes was buried directly under the hidden concrete dummies. If the mines were not correctly lifted then the thunder flashes would be triggered and the whole lot would explode upwards and you were lying within eyeball range of these mines. It was bloody scary. In daylight hours clearing a minefield of both types of mine was no fun, but wars are not necessarily conducted in daylight hours, and so we had to learn to do all this at night. In the dark and in wet and inhospitable weather, this made the whole business a very fraught experience indeed. At least one sapper on one of our night exercise suffered a broken jaw as an anti-tank mine exploded in his face. Clearing minefields is not for the faint hearted. Mine detectors were available but the technology was not guaranteed and sappers had to learn the basics i.e. how to do it the hard way. The other 'fun part' of this course was the use of, and the neutralising of, booby traps. These were small explosive devices (again thunder flashes) that would be hidden in a room and triggered to explode if not correctly de-activated. Even entering the booby-trapped room was cause for concern - was the door or window booby-trapped or not? … and so it went on. Chairs were carefully inspected, windows checked and everything that moved was given a careful once over. This was never quite so dangerous as the mine warfare, but it was still nerve racking. As always, the NCOs managed to lay a few traps that you never suspected and so one never escaped 'Scot free'. Directly after this we had demolitions, which were carried out on an army training area reasonably close to our camp. The training area, which was extensive, resembled nothing more than a blasted heath pock marked with large depressions in the ground; the result of many tank trap explosive charges having been set off. Here we had great fun preparing various types of charges using various types of explosives. Blowing great craters in the ground using buried charges and blowing holes through two inch steel plates using a bit of kit known as a 'Beehive'. The 'Beehive' stood about 12" tall and about 6" in diameter. The top half was a steel cylinder packed with explosive and the bottom half was an inverted cone to target the explosion in the direction of the axis of the cone. It worked beautifully.

It was at the start of this period of training on demolitions and booby traps that two other soldiers had joined us. Smartly turned out and able to do all the drills etc without a second thought - but it was the demolition and booby trap training that they were keenly interested in. Who were these guys, we wondered, that could suddenly join our troop without having gone through the earlier training? The fact that they wore what appeared like inverted Para wings on their right shoulder meant nothing to us. It was not until some time later that we learned that they had been sappers and were now with the SAS doing extra refresher training, and had already been in the army for at least three years.

Interspersed with all of our military duties we also had the delights of the gym to look forward to. 3TRRE had a particularly large well-equipped gym. So it was that the drill instructors pushed everyone to their personal limits on all the many exercises that were designed to find the collapse point of every muscle in your body. It was during these exercises that, like the drying room sessions, you had to show resolve and no sign of weakness. Any indications that you were flagging would be the trigger point for more abuse to be inflicted upon you, although it would have to be said that the drill instructors were somewhat more temperate in their language than our NCOs.

It was also those same drill instructors that introduced us to the assault course. This was particularly beneficial since those early rounds of the course were done wearing just our PT shorts and plimsolls. It was only after we had been instructed in the correct methods of tackling the assault course that we then had the much more difficult task of doing the needful in Battle Order, tin hat and rifle. Fortunately, the tin hat was worn on the back of the backpack; otherwise you would never have had any hope of completing the course in any sort of sensible time frame. It goes without saying that the Royal Engineers had constructed the assault course, and it seemed to us that the designer of the course had had a particularly warped mind - which is another way of saying it was not an easy course. In the main it was fashioned from slim tree trunks or logs, from which the bark had long gone, with the result that in the winter months, such as we were experiencing, the timbers got particularly slippy and icy. The climbing sections and ropes were OK, but jumping from one log or bar to the next, at height, was particularly fraught. One lived in expectations that you might just land legs akimbo either side of one of the logs, and fully weighted down by your kit. Not many sappers enjoyed the thought if that happening to them.

I think it was watermanship that followed mine warfare. We were now into November/December but fortunately we could expect to arrive at Hawley Lake to find that the admin. squad had done their sterling work as far as ice breaking was concerned. We learnt to paddle assault boats, row cutters with 15' oars (hard work) and power metal pontoons, again using oars. Close Support Rafts (CSRs) were built. These consisted of two pontoons held together by a small bridge section. All of this had to be built in double quick time. I don't think the army was aware of any other time scale. These CSRs could carry a small TCV or other light vehicle and were usually driven by a small on-board motor, or on occasions, by poling by hand. All these skills then had to be practiced at night, or on over-night exercises. You could never expect to complete one of the exercises without getting sodden clothes. You just had to hope that it would be towards the end of the exercise when you could get back to camp to change into dry clothing, but 'Sod' usually thought otherwise. In better weather this would all have been great fun, but in the depths of winter it was no such thing. On most night exercises over the winter months it was de-rigueur to wear your pyjamas underneath your denims to add another layer of clothing in an effort to keep warm, and it was normally very successful in this regard, except for the times that you ended 'in the drink'. Then your extra layers of clothing became a waterlogged mass which soon had an adverse effect on the thermal properties of your apparel e.g. it all became bloody cold, heavy and uncomfortable.

During one of our exercises we had to assemble a raft from some canvas skinned boats and then pole our way around a particular course that had been set out. As it transpired, the wind rose in strength to such an extent that we could not complete the course and we got blown off the route by a considerable margin. The result was that a powerboat had to be launched to rescue us, but such was the strength of the wind that even with it towing us we still got into difficulties. It was only when the wind abated that we were able to get back to terra firma. It was also at this time that on another part of the lake two sappers got blown off the boat they were on and into the drink. This was a particularly unpleasant experience at this late time of the year.

The other skill that we had to learn during this part of our training was that of learning to tie knots and lashes, which was particularly necessary for the lashing of floating pontoons. Regrettably, I have to say, I have now forgotten most of the knots and lashes that I learnt at that time, but I suppose that is not unreasonable after a passage of nearly six decades. It was sometime around this period that we got out of camp for the first time, but only down to the local pub - the Crown and Cushion - which was located about half a mile from the barracks. It was a brief sojourn and the place was packed with similarly unleashed sappers.

Following on from watermanship came Bailey Bridging - another vital part of the skill set of the Royal Engineer. Most of this this training was again carried out at Hawley Lake. Bailey bridges were built, dismantled and re-built, all in double quick time over inlets at the south-eastern corner of the lake. We had to build these bridges - simple constructions to start with - as quickly as humanly possible. A considerable amount of energy was spent on this work. Each Bailey Panel was considered to be a six-man load and so teamwork was essential in the lifting and manoeuvring of these steel panels. All panels were fixed to the adjacent panels by steel pins approximately two inch in diameter and about six inches long. Accuracy was important in placing and driving home these pins into the appropriate joint. As a consequence, it was best to do this with your bare hands to enable a better grip of the pins; unfortunately, in the depths of winter the pins might stick to your hands, such was the prevailing temperature. Speed was always of the essence, but in the prevailing conditions it was more than a little too easy to drop a pin, but this rarely happened. The philosophy prevailing was that if you dropped a pin, then you were tasked with retrieving it from the icy waters of the lake - a most difficult and unpleasant task - particularly when on a night exercise. Naturally, very few dropped a pin. However, it also meant that sappers were particularly careful when placing the pins into the appropriate holes in the panels. This meant that more time was expended than a corporal was prepared to tolerate as he witnessed this apparently slow process. *Sapper, move yourself. If it had hair around it you'd get it in quick enough* was one of many exhortations that you could expect to hear. In the pitch dark of night exercises it was often difficult to locate the hole into which the pin had to be inserted. *Sapper, use your weekend finger; you'll find it soon enough.* One could only laugh...

After we had mastered the construction of single panel bridges we were soon on to double panel height constructions and extra wide Bailey Bridges. That this work was fatiguing was a gross understatement. Many were the sappers that suffered from back strain in later life due to the continual lifting of these heavy bits of kit in the cold and damp, even wet, conditions.

The assault courses, already mentioned, were another part of the training that we had to undertake at regular intervals with the aim being to be able to traverse the course at greater and greater speed every time it was attempted. As I have mentioned earlier, slipping on some of the obstacles with legs akimbo could only result in untold horrors. It did not bear thinking about.

Then there was *Operation Knockout.* I cannot recall when this took place during our basic training, but I think it was in the first few weeks. As far as I am aware this was an exercise that was scheduled to take place over the whole of the Aldershot Garrison Area. The thinking behind the plan was that a nuclear device had been exploded somewhere in the region and that all normal aspects of life had been neutralised. So, when the alert was given, the whole camp had to get fully kitted up in Field Service Marching Order, the barracks area made secure, and the whole camp mobilised within a 30-minute period. Thereafter, the camp had to be evacuated and the regiment transported to an assigned destination. We seemed to practice forever for this alert. It was now that the practising we had done early on in our training regarding quick kit changes began to bear fruit. Of course, we could never do it quick enough for the 'Lance Jack' in charge of our room; but we did make very good attempts such that there was much shouting and screaming at us, but nothing that warranted any disciplinary reaction. Clearly, we were improving.

The day dawned when the alarm was given - a day that we had been rather fearful of. As it so happened all our practising and training bore fruit and the whole exercise went off very smoothly indeed. Our camp commander was delighted; it was even rumoured that Brigade Commander had been impressed, but of that we had no official confirmation.

Based on my educational qualifications I had been graded 'potential officer' at Merebrook Camp and this was no doubt one of the reasons for my posting to No. 3TRRE. But as the potential officers in our party very soon found out this was a dubious honour. Any epithet that hinted at potential officer, officer cadet, or similar, meant that for the duration you were a target for the NCOs who were going to maximise their authority whilst it still prevailed. Once you had been graded thus, you were expected to achieve higher standards than the other trainees; and the corporals did not let you forget it. A similar, but less harsh regime also existed for those that had been graded as potential NCOs. Everything had to be done that bit better. It meant of course that duties such as Room Senior were delegated more often to those that were graded into either of these two categories. I was fortunate that the room I was in had a very good group of sappers who, by and large, were willing to play their part in anything that came their way. Consequently, when I was Room Senior we managed to win the 'best room' competition on a few occasions - something that always pleased the room 'Lance Jack'. It has to be said that I was not too displeased myself. Again, when on exercises and at other times, potential officers and potential NCOs would be given extra duties to carry out - perhaps the supervision and execution of some modest task or other. Naturally, the Party Officer, the Sergeant and NCOs monitored these duties assiduously to check on the qualities of the candidate with a view to deciding whether or not you might progress further in the selection process towards your designated potential. At No. 3TRRE this was a rigorous selection process.

After the first four weeks or thereabouts of your time at Guillemont Barracks the Party Officer interviewed all those who had been graded potential officer. In an intake of 100 sappers this could be expected to be somewhere between zero and 15 candidates. This interview was normally in the region of 45-60 minutes long. The topics covered were wide ranging and nothing was excluded. A wide knowledge of the political events of the day in the UK was expected, including a decent awareness of what was happening in other countries. The un-said recommendation was that it was necessary to read the quality broadsheets in your free time [sic] to be abreast of current affairs. Money for these papers to be read on Sunday was in short supply, as was the time at your disposal to do so. Sharing of broadsheets was common to minimise the financial outlay. Other matters covered would be your hobbies and outside interests and anything the candidate or the Party Officer wished to discuss. If you wanted to progress in the selection process it was always a good plan to be able to initiate other topics to be discussed during the interview. Afterwards the Party Officer would then write a report on the candidate and include in it his observations on your progress in training thus far, and your competence in dealing with the various responsibilities that you had been allocated during your training. The report was concluded with his recommendations as to your suitability for further progress in the selection process. All reports were then passed to the officer commanding the squadron (OC) for his action. This officer carried the rank of major. A week or two later the candidate would then be summoned to an interview with the OC for another grilling. If the interview lasted 30 minutes or less then it could usually be assumed that the OC had decided that the candidate was not suitable material and no further time would be wasted with the interview. A longer interview of about 45-60 minutes did not mean success, but it did mean that the OC was giving consideration to the potential of the candidate. After a discussion with the Party Officer on the further progress that the candidate had made in his training the OC would then decide on each candidate's application. Of a batch of say fifteen candidates, which would have been a likely maximum for a large party, all would have been allowed to progress from the Party Officer's interview to the OC's interview.

From this a maximum of three or four might have been expected to progress to an interview with the commanding officer (CO) - a Lieutenant Colonel - a week or two later. The OC's selection was rigorous because the commanding officer was extremely fussy about putting candidates forward for selection if he did not think they would make the grade. The CO's interview was usually a shorter affair of around 30 minutes. He made up his mind very quickly and if there was any doubt that you were marginal or not suitable, then it was 'curtains for you'. From the three or four that the OC has passed for interview the CO could be expected to reduce this to one or perhaps two. I was fortunate in that the CO decided that I should be allowed to progress to the next stage in the selection process, i.e. The War Office Selection Board (WOSB). At any stage, if you did not pass the selection process for potential officer, then you continued with your basic training for a posting in due course. If you were fortunate enough to get the colonel's recommendation for further progression then basic training continued, but you were placed in the queue to attend WOSB. This could normally be expected to happen towards the end of your basic training.

By now it was nearly the end of December 1957. A letter home to Lorna at the end of that month put everything in a nutshell;

...nothing here to bring Christmas to our attention except the date on the calendar.

1958

War Office Selection Board

When you were due to attend WOSB you were given a travel warrant and told to report at a given date and time at Barton Stacey Camp near Andover. This was some distance from our camp and involved two train changes as I recollect, and a hike to the camp from the station. No transport was laid on - perhaps you were expected to have the taxi fare! Potential officers were clearly expected to be self-sufficient. I arrived there on Tuesday 7 January 1958 for the selection process through to Friday 10 January. A week prior to this our Party at No. 3TRRE had had the luxury of 5 days Christmas leave, which was hugely enjoyable, but arriving as it did just before WOSB rather took the shine off it because my mind kept returning to the selection process that immediately lay ahead. I do not remember how many candidates attended these selection courses, but I would have guessed in the region of 50 - 100 at a time. The interviews started all over again, but this time in greater depth and with two or more officers grilling you at each session. The topics were all inclusive, but political awareness was high on the agenda. Then there were the lectures and lecturettes. For the lecturettes a small group of candidates would be assembled in a room and then randomly, the officers in attendance would select a candidate and throw him an object - say a matchbox, or some other inconsequential object - and invite [sic] him to speak for four minutes on the object in question. You had to be quick on your feet, so to speak, to be able to talk about these random objects about which, you had been given no prior warning. Then there were the other lectures. For these you would be given a topic, and a few hours warning, but no preparation time, then you would again be invited [sic] to deliver a ten to fifteen minute lecture. And, of course, there was your main lecture. Prior to going to WOSB you would be told that you would be asked to give a fifteen minute lecture on any topic of your choice. For this my mind had gone blank and even although I had been given sufficient notice I could think of nothing that I wanted to talk about. I had even asked Lorna to send me some literature from home relating to the Edinburgh International Festival of Music & Drama. But I was not enthused and could work up no appetite for this subject matter. WOSB duly arrived and I had still not settled on a lecture topic - panic was beginning to creep in. But luck was on my side. After arriving at Andover and before going onto Barton Stacey Camp I had some time to kill and when wandering around Andover I chanced upon a second hand bookshop. A quick browse around the shop delivered my saving grace. They had a very slim pamphlet - about 10-20 pages long on the *International Geophysical Year*, which was then currently taking place between 1 July 1957 and 31 December 1958. This was right up my street. I was interested in astronomy and some of the earth sciences that were being researched by many nations during this period. I sure as hell hoped that no one would know anything about the *International Geophysical Year*. I had a whole two days to refresh my memory about the event and memorise the most technical phrases that I could muster - at least I could bore them to death so that no one would ask any awkward questions. The ploy worked reasonably well - no one appeared to have heard of the *International Geophysical Year* and everyone seemed totally bemused. The upside of their bemusement meant there were no awkward questions - so far, so good. At least it had been different from the other lectures that had been delivered.

Then we had various assault courses that we had to navigate to be assessed on our fitness and flexibility. Thereafter, small groups of candidates were given tasks that we had to carry out. The invigilators would separate the intake into small groups of five or six persons and then give each member of the team a task to be completed by the team. This was designed to see how each member could assimilate the situation and quickly devise a solution to the problem; and then organise the team to carry out the allotted task within a given time frame. This was more difficult than might have been thought possible. Each member of the team was someone who was under supervision and who wanted to show his leadership skills to the best advantage. Consequently, few were willing to do as they were bid, each wanted to have his say and lead the team, irrespective of whether or not it was his responsibility. Tempers could get quite fraught. Task were varied, but something such as the team transporting a barrel over a 50 or 60 foot gap which also contained an obstacle of some not inconsequential height. The barrel and team would have to negotiate this without the barrel, or the team, touching the intervening ground. Planks of wood, bits of rope and other sundry items would be provided to assist in the operation - which had a finite time for completion. It was then that you found out that 'Sod' had been at work. Why was it that your team was a bunch of independently minded useless twats - usually from some cavalry regiment? Perhaps that is too harsh, but it felt like that at the time.

Then there were the written situational problems that you would be presented with. In the lecture room you were given blank paper and pencil and presented with a theoretical situational problem to which, in the allotted time, you had to present your solution on paper, and in a logical manner, giving the reasons for the various decisions and actions that you had proposed. You had more than problem one to solve, or at least arrive at a best possible solution, because not all were totally solvable. The problems were normally of a military nature, but many was the candidate that had to propose the best method of rescuing Rapunzel from her 50 foot tower, after first negotiating some military defences, and with nothing to aid you.

In between the physical activities a few Intelligence Tests had to be negotiated. Thus, the days passed very quickly and all the time the invigilators were watching like a hawk to see how the candidates fared. It was assumed that each night the invigilators assembled to discuss the day's events and award marks to the various candidates for their efforts throughout the day.

Late on the afternoon of the last day all the candidates would be assembled and notices were posted to indicate a Pass, or Fail, or Referral for each person. A Pass was just that. A Fail was also just that, with no possibility of a second attempt at a later date. A Referral was an uncommon outcome and was reserved for a candidate that the examiners thought was satisfactory, but was perhaps a little too immature, or not of sufficient experience to pass, but who were nevertheless thought worthy of a second attempt six months later. For national service candidates this was not a feasible option as they had too little time to serve after the waiting period to make it worth the army's time to train such a candidate. So, referrals were normally reserved for those hoping to gain a short-term commission. The pass rate was normally around 25% Pass and 75% Fail with only a very few being graded as a Referral. I was very lucky and surprised myself by passing. From 3TRRE and my intake of just over 100 sappers we had six candidates sent to WOSB - an unusually high number. Of the six, three passed the selection board - again, a high percentage for one intake.

Now was the time for serious reflection. Did we really want to try for a commission? We three sappers knew that what had gone before was nothing to what we could expect over the next many months. The tales about our next posting - Mons Officer Cadet School - were well known to us, but after that lay three months at Gordon Barracks in Gillingham - close to the headquarters of the Royal Engineers. The stories that emanated about this posting were fearsome. Guillemont Barracks had been but a preparation for what we were about to experience.

When we returned to camp from WOSB, myself and the two other sappers who had passed were immediately transferred to Pre OCS (Pre Officer Cadet School) and the other three sappers returned to our party. As it so happened Pre OCS was also located at No. 3TRRE, so we had barely a few hundred yards to walk to our new billet. Pre OCS was in fact merely a holding troop where you were posted until the next intake at Mons Officer Cadet School. Nevertheless, the powers that be had decreed that your time in this troop would not be wasted and that every effort was made to prepare you for Mons. As luck would have it I was only in this troop about two weeks before my posting to Mons was finalised.

In Pre OCS the distinguishing feature that singled you out from other soldiers was the fact that you wore a white circular disc behind your cap badge; a feature that was to continue throughout the remainder of our officer cadet training. Drill was still an essential part of our training, and now that you were a cadet your standard was expected to be better than ever before, so what was new? But drilling only occupied a small proportion of our time. Things now started to get much more interesting. Training in navigation followed, i.e. map reading and marching on compass bearings etc. Naturally, this could not go without the mandatory night scheme where we had to navigate over large tracts of army land; land that had previously been used for tank training. At night these training areas, which extended for many miles, resembled nothing more than a bleak moonscape, and featureless with it. Consequently, navigation depended entirely upon your skill with the compass and to have total confidence in your ability to use this little instrument. Many were the cadets that got lost - not surprisingly - and search parties would have to be mounted to find these lost cadets.

Then there were the initiative tests. For these exciting ploys you would be assembled early in a morning kitted out in your battle dress and second best boots. Once our small group assembled, because there were only about six or seven of us cadets in Pre OCS, we would be checked over by the officer in charge to ensure that we had no money, or maps, or anything of use on our person before the exercise started. Each cadet was then given their orders for the day and ushered onto a TCV, which had been blanked out to ensure that you could see nothing of where you were going. Travelling with us was an NCO to ensure that no attempt was made to have a sneaky peak from under the canvass tarpaulin of the vehicle. The TCV (Troop Carrying Vehicle) would then set off on a mazy journey through the countryside for approximately two hours to ensure that you were a considerable distance from camp - usually about 50 miles or so. Along the way, at various deserted spots, a cadet would be decanted to carry out his orders, which up to that time he had not been allowed to open. The basic task was of course to make your way back to camp using your own wiles and there was always a time limit which was something like 9.00 or 10.00 p.m. in the evening. But that alone was considered too easy by far. En-route back to camp you were tasked with a number of things to do, such as get the postal stamp from a designated village post office which was always somewhere you had never heard of, or get the autograph of a well known personality who lived in a particular area. Remember, this was in the Thames Valley/Home Counties region and at that time film starlets and media personalities abounded; or get the inscription from the War Memorial in some remote spot, again unheard of. Naturally, this had to be memorised because you had no paper or pencil. Most, if not all of us cadets were from distant parts, so the geography of the Home Counties was unknown to most of us. Getting a postal stamp from the local postmistress was not a problem, if only you could find the village. Autographs were decidedly more difficult. You could waste precious time trying to find out who the local personalities were, and then Sod would intervene again - they would not be at home just when you needed them most. Local inscriptions were easy, if only you knew where this remote community was located - many miles from the last it would transpire. Time and distance was always your enemy. You had to rely a great deal on being able to hitch a lift to the next destination on your list. Fortunately, in the 1950s, soldiers in uniform were a common sight everywhere in the Southern Command Area and drivers of vehicles of all types were normally willing to give someone in uniform a lift, assuming they were heading in a common direction. Nontheless, getting back to camp in the allotted time with all the tasks completed consumed all the time available. Meals were something that you had to forgo unless you were able to cadge something en-route. I don't recollect what we did for food when we returned to camp because by that time the cookhouse had closed - the NAAFI, I presume.

More weapon training was another activity we got to indulge ourselves in, but this time it was a bit more personal as there were so few of us. And to keep us on our toes we had a day on the para assault course in Aldershot that had gained a bit of a reputation. As it turned out it was not any harder than what we had encountered at 3TRRE, but it was different being somewhat higher and constructed mainly from scaffold poles. In all probability it had likely been built by some sapper troop.

As it was, the short time we had at Pre OCS turned out to be rather enjoyable. Discipline was strict and standards were high, but everything was just a bit more relaxed. We had passed WOSB and were destined for Mons; this was but a brief interlude in our training before the months of hard sweat ahead. On the 21st January 1958 we three cadets reunited with our squadron for the last time to prepare to take part in the 'Passing off Parade', which went rather well. Passing off to the sound of 'Wings', the Royal Engineers regimental march was quite exhilarating. We were now sappers. As was normal, we now had seven days leave to look forward to before we took up our various postings. In my case, to Mon OCS for another six weeks of more advanced infantry training.

But before that seven days of bliss lay ahead. In effect the seven days was in reality five days, because two days were spent travelling. By the time the 'Pass off Parade' and all the attendant farewells had been said it was well into the afternoon/evening period, then you had to assemble all your kit and make your way to Farnborough Station to catch the first available train to

Waterloo. But before that there was one more duty to perform. With great glee the 'Passing Out' party would seek out the newest intake they could find, and then goad them with the call *how many more days to 'Pass Off' you sprogs?* The tension of fourteen weeks training was being released.

Once at Waterloo I then had to make my way across London to Kings Cross to get the train north to Edinburgh. At both Waterloo and Kings Cross you had to be on guard for the 'Red Caps' - the military police who were always more than happy to apprehend any soldier, particularly one that looked like a new recruit, if they thought that you or your kit was not up to a sufficient standard. If apprehended, you could expect a long inquisition and consequent delay in your travel timings, which more often than not would mean a missed connection - something to be avoided at all costs. Make sure you were 'up to scratch' was always good motto to follow because on these quick fire inspections the 'Red Caps' would try to find every fault with your turnout. If I was lucky, I could just make *The Talisman* express to Edinburgh: departing 4.00 p.m. from Kings Cross and arriving 10.40 p.m. Edinburgh Waverley. If I missed that one then the next train did not get into Edinburgh until 3.43 a.m., which was a bit of a 'bummer'. These trains were always packed with servicemen going home on leave and because I could never get to Kings Cross early enough to get a seat, it normally meant a long stand in the corridor for the nearly seven hour journey, unless one was lucky enough to get a seat at York or Newcastle when many decanted. I have no notes for that period of leave but I'm sure every hour was filled to the full in Lorna's company. At the end of the leave it was the usual heart-breaking parting. This time it was a Wednesday afternoon departure with Waverley Station again looking quiet and bleak, as were our spirits. Mons OCS and the unknown beckoned.

Mons Officer Cadet School, Mons Barracks, Aldershot, Hampshire

Mons Officer Cadet School was located within the Aldershot Garrison Area and was the training camp for potential officers in the Royal Engineers, the Royal Artillery, the Tank Corp, the cavalry regiments and cadets from the other technical regiments. It was also the Officer Cadet School for regular army officers undertaking a short service commission. The equivalent training camp for potential officers for the infantry battalions was at the stately mansion of Eaton Hall, which was located near to Chester. This building was later demolished in 1963 due to the extent of repairs necessary to bring it up to habitable standards. It was commonly accepted that the training regime at Mons was somewhat harder than the one at Eaton Hall. This was generally attributed to the fact that Mons OCS was located within the heartland of the British army and was commanded by a very senior British officer, and disciplined by one of the most senior regimental sergeant majors in the British army. In the spring of 1958 Eaton Hall OCS was closed down and subsumed into the Mons OCS establishment.

Prior to my arrival at Mons the regimental sergeant major had been RSM Ronald Brittain MBE, MSM (he of the loudest voice in the army), but he retired in 1954 and RSM Charles L Smy MBE, DCM, took over his position. Then, in the spring of 1958, when Eaton Hall OCS was closed down RSM Desmond T Lynch MBE, DCM took over from RSM Smy who was leaving the army. Richard Alford, writing in *To Revel in God's Sunshine*, described RSM Lynch as *one of the very top league of RSMs in the British Army.* However, it was during the transitional period between RSM Smy departing and RSM Lynch becoming fully embedded into Mons OCS that RSM J C Lord MVO, MBE carried out very occasional inspection parades at Mons. RSM J C Lord was at that time the most senior RSM in the British Army and was the Regimental Sergeant Major at the Royal Military

Academy at Sandhurst, which was not far distant from Mons. RSM Lord was also the demonstrator for the rifle drill movements in the *Army Drill Manual.* Around 1960 his rank of Regimental Sergeant Major was upgraded to Academy Sergeant Major. At the Royal Military Academy it was reputed that RSM Lord had admonished King Hussein of Jordan, who was undergoing military training, with the reproof; *you idle little Monarch, Sir.* He was also known to frequently reproof the king with the comment *Mr King of Jordan Sir, pull on your rifle butt.* Provided the prefix, or suffix, 'Sir' was used; it was permissible to address a cadet in such a manner. He was also given to tell new cadets that JC (Jesus Christ) was the Lord up there, pointing his pace stick skywards, and that he was the Lord down here, grounding his pace stick once again. He was not a character to be messed about. He was a soldier through and through.

At Mons all the NCOs were senior regular army soldiers. They expected nothing less than the best you could provide and we soon found that the oft-stated comment that at Mons you had to *bull the bull* was pretty near the truth.

Mons was the same as No. 3TRRE - wooden spiders sleeping a similar numbers of cadets. I'm not sure what the size of an intake at Mons was, but I reckon it was somewhere in the region of 50 or 60 cadets at a time. Like No. 3TRRE, there were no radiators in the rooms, just a small potboiler (I think), and it was bloody cold. The time we were to spend at Mons was to be six weeks doing advanced infantry training. Now, in addition to the white disc behind our cap badges we also had to wear white gorget tabs on the collars of our battle dress. This certainly made you more noticeable, but it had the advantage of enhancing the appearance of the British battle dress, which was made of particularly drab and rough looking serge. A lot of the cadets were a different class of person to whom I had been used to associating with, but I did not find that troublesome as I felt I could get along with most types. As I wrote home after just arriving at Mons; *a lot of the cadets seem very pukka pukka types with money to spend, a bit of a change from normal. But they are all nice guys.*

Training was varied and consisted of lectures, both giving and receiving. Whilst we were being pumped full of military tactics, military organisation and military law, we also had to give lectures, again the 10 min variety, on any of a host of topics under the sun. The fun part was the 'platoon attacks' where each cadet in turn had to command a platoon on many different exercises attacking or defending positions, as the invigilators saw fit. Having been given a platoon and told what the attack target was, you were left to assess the situation and then brief the platoon on the tactics you had devised, and then have that tactic executed to achieve the objective. Naturally, with a platoon of potential officers each wanted to have their say, and do it their way. One had to be firm, if not positively abusive, to ensure that they did it your way. But of course the invigilators knew that any fool could plan a suitable tactic given time, and so they would allow you to progress with your master plan and then when you had reached a critical stage in the operation they would immediately announce a change in the military parameters. The invigilator would increase the enemy from a troop to a company of soldiers and they would no longer be located ahead of you, they would be transposed to behind your lines and closing fast. The ploy of course was to see who could react sensibly and quickly to a fast changing situation and redeploy your platoon to still achieve the original objective. Naturally, things could go disastrously wrong and often did. On one of my particular exercises when the parameters were changed suddenly and drastically I managed to kill off most of my platoon, other than a few souls and myself, although the end objective was achieved. Unsurprisingly, the 'deceased' members of the platoon were not at all happy at having to play dead when they wanted to be showing off their officer like qualities.

Unfortunately, it was January through February/March when we were 'enjoying' these outside activities and often the snow was lying about five to six inches thick on many of the training areas. Crawling through the snow for long periods of time with a Bren gun or a Lee Enfield, and kitted out in full battle order and firing off rounds of blanks, was not particularly appealing. It meant that for the whole day you were sodden from top to toe, but it was essential that you put a brave face on the situation. Anything less and you would have been on your way out the door.

At this time we also had the pleasure of repeating the night exercise that we had had in basic training - that of retrieving a guarded lit lantern, albeit over different ground. The main difference this time was that we were now crawling long distances through snow and sodden grass rather than mud. The joys were never ending!

Combined with the platoon exercises were the night schemes of a similar nature, but even colder and more miserable. One would have been grateful for more that one layer of pyjamas under the denims. For some reason one of the exercises was code-named *Bolonia* - why, I don't know. In addition to these night schemes were the navigational ones carrying out more mapping and navigation by compass. The training area for these exercises looked the same as the ones we had used when at Pre OCS, but who could tell? The whole landscape was featureless other than the chewed up underfoot conditions. It could have been any moon in the solar system. Under the climatic conditions prevailing at the time it was one of the exercise when you endeavoured to do your very best. It was not an appealing prospect to entertain the thought of getting lost on the vast training area. Help would not have arrived until sometime the following day. One could get very cold and hungry in the intervening period. Fortunately, I don't recollect any search parties having to be mounted for lost cadets.

Our indoor activities were no less exciting. To enable the invigilators to determine those who had a bit of spunk and determination we had boxing matches. On these occasions the PT staff would line up the cadets and pair them off with another cadet of similar height and build. You then had to go three two-minute rounds, or was it two three-minute rounds (?) with your sparring partner. Collusion between the pairs to land soft blows on each other was something the invigilators were fully aware of and meant a negative assessment. Once one cadet had landed a hard blow to his opponent then it was hammer and tongs all the way. There was always much flailing of fists and a great degree of energy expended, but very little boxing skill was shown. Many were the red eyes, bruises, and aches and pains, but never any hard feelings between opponents. But the next time you knew you were going to get him back for that 'smack in the chops' he had landed on you.

At Mons, leave was decidedly more generous than had previously been the case. Most weekends you were allowed out of camp between last parade Friday and first parade Monday. Naturally, you had to make sure that you had all your kit 'bulled up' and your exam revision up-to-date before availing yourself of this luxury. For most cadets they either did not have the funds to go home on leave at these times or alternatively, home was too distant to entertain the thought. In my case both restrictions applied, so most weekends were spent in camp; but there was a hidden benefit to this. Most of the cavalry types appeared to live within the catchment area of the Home Counties and had money to get home. Ergo, they wanted to go home as often as duties would allow. Guard duties were usually the main restriction that prohibited their going home over a weekend; so it was that many of us camp bound, financially poor cadets, could make 'a little bit on the side' by volunteering to do their 24-hour guard duty for them. As I recall, the going rate was 10/-. Ten shillings in old money is 50 pence in today's currency; but at that time it was good money - approx. a third of the army weekly wage. The extra income meant that on the very few occasions, when time permitted, we could visit the nearby Frensham Ponds Hotel to imbibe of the local brew. In that particular era the Frensham Ponds Hotel was a very desirable 'hot spot' for the county set.

It was on one of these money-earning extra guard duties for a cadet-colleague that very nearly ended my time at Mons. Sometime prior to the weekend I had been feeling decidedly grotty and slowly developed what appeared to be a boil, or something more serious, on my left arm. As the weekend grew closer the boil grew ever larger such that it clearly wasn't a boil but some rather large protuberance on my arm. By the time the weekend arrived and I was due to go on parade in the evening I was feeling decidedly unwell, and as luck would have it, there was no one else that was available to swop duties with me. All the remaining cadets in camp were already committed in some way or other. Now, it was the case that in the army you could only report sick at 8.00 a.m. in the morning by reporting to the medical room in your second BD and great coat, having already packed some of your kit into your small pack and deposited in the Quartermaster's store. However, I was by now in such a grotty state that I hurriedly found out where the medical room was, and without the formality of depositing my small pack at the Quartermaster's store I presented myself to the orderly corporal on duty and reported my condition, stating that I had to be on guard duty at 6.00 p.m. that evening, come what may. It did not take long for him to assess the problem and in his wisdom decided that the whole protuberance had to be lanced there and then. The prospect did not appeal one bit but I was too far-gone to worry one way or the other. So, after cleaning and preparing my arm out came a very large scalpel to do the needful. It was then that a rather imposing figure who had been seated in a chair in the corner of the room, but to whom I had paid little attention, rose and came over to inspect what was going on. It was RSM Lord on one of his occasional visits to Mons during the transitional period of Eaton Hall OCS moving to Mons OCS - but frankly I didn't care. The lancing duly took place and I could feel all during the procedure that I was drifting in and out of consciousness. RSM Lord surveyed the scene with a decided grimace and soon went back to his seat in the corner of the room. The lancing completed and the wound bandaged up I left the medical centre in a very woozy state being barely able to walk straight, such that I crashed into the door of the medical centre on my way out which brought me to my knees. I just managed to get myself upright before the medical orderly had dashed over to offer assistance. By the time it was time to get ready for guard duty I had recovered a little, but only a little. I assembled all my kit and got ready for the parade but I had a major problem - even greater than my medical condition; I could not find the bolt to my rifle. Bolt and rifle were always kept in two separate locations for security. There was nothing for it I just had to be on parade no matter what, so I trooped off to the shed where the parade took place. This was still February/March so the nights were dark and the shed was very dimly lit. Could I get away with it I wondered, so I took the precaution of positioning myself in the middle rank of the guard - any port in a storm? By this time I was beginning to drift in and out of any state of awareness and could barely keep my composure. To my horror it turned out that RSM Lord was the inspecting officer that evening - *bloody hell, I'm on the way out of Mons and the army for sure.* The parade passed off reasonably well and then when I thought I might just be getting away with murder the RSM instructed the guard commander to line us up for rifle inspection. F***, the s*** had hit the fan! Lord slowly made his way around the ranks, not once did he indicate that he would look at any rifle, surely I thought I've slipped the net again - but no. He sombrely made his way to me and then tapped my Lee Enfield with his pace stick. This was the sign to port arms and present the rifle barrel for inspection. In a decidedly groggy condition I duly went through the procedure of raising the rifle and pulling the bolt back to let the light enter the barrel for inspection; but of course there was no bolt. I was merely going through the drill and fooling no one, least of all RSM Lord. Lord duly inspected the barrel, which I knew was spotless and then gave the command to return to attention. When was he going to erupt like Vesuvius? Surely he would not let this pass with out some terrible retribution. But no, he dismissed the guard and we were duly marched back to the Guard Room by the guard commander - and RSM Lord followed us back. Now, he was going to descend like the proverbial ton of bricks when we entered the Guard Room. I couldn't believe my ears when, as we got into the guardroom, I overheard the RSM say to the Guard Commander *send that cadet to his bed for the first stag*. Hells bells, I couldn't believe it. Thank the Lord seemed more than a little inadequate, although entirely appropriate for the occasion. I managed to get through the rest of that guard duty but it was more by good luck and will power than anything else. I was certainly in no fit state to engage any intruder should they appear.

Engaging intruders was uppermost in our minds, because earlier in the month the IRA had made an attempt to steal weapons from an REME depot in Blandford in Dorset. It was thought that they had targeted the base because they had some inside information from an IRA sympathiser who worked at the camp. The consequence was that we, and all other camps in Southern Command were on High Alert for a repeat attack. Indeed, on a few guard duties during this state of High Alert the guard platoons were issued with live rounds for their rifles, although I cannot remember what instructions we were given regarding their use. However, my troubles were not yet over; I had still lost my rifle bolt, which was a very serious offence. It was at least 24 hours later before I found it. Fortunately, in that intervening period I had not had any duty that required the use of a rifle. Was I lucky, or was I not? Apart from that upset things went reasonably well at Mons. Discipline was strict but not unfair, and standards were very high, but our time at 3TRRE had prepared us well for this; more so it seemed than the majority of cadets from the other regiments - many of whom were really struggling with the 'bull' and discipline.

As we neared the end or our time at Mons we started to get more and more exams on various topics including Military Law,

Military Organisation and Military Tactics and it was necessary to pass all of the exams if one wanted to progress further. By then we had noticed that at various times throughout the course cadets would disappear never to return. They had not made it this far. We did not want to join them so the midnight oil was burned long into the night.

Also, towards the end of the Mons training course we had an 'At Home'. This was in fact an exercise for us cadets to organise, and hold, a cocktail party to entertain the regular officers in our Training Company. This was not my thing and was a task that I did not particularly look forward to. It was reputed to be an informal affair and that the officers would not be looking for gentlemanlike qualities in us, or giving us marks for our presentation, personal and otherwise - but we were never sure. It was best to pull out all the stops as we only had a short time to go till 'Pass Off'. As it turned out the evening went rather well and there was no hint of officiousness, or of appraisals being secretly carried out.

The last weekend in camp turned out to be rather a bore. There was some holiday or other that I do not recollect, but the whole camp was on a 36-hour pass. Some of us had neither the time, or the money, or both, to get home so it we spent it in camp; and to make matters worse the NAAFI was shut as well. The weekend did, however, give time to catch up on some well-needed sleep, because immediately prior to this we had not been able to get to bed before 3.00 a.m. most days due to our workload.

Tuesday 4 March 1958 dawned bright and clear and the 'Pass off Parade' duly took place with some Major General taking the salute. It turned out that he was impressed by our display, which meant of course that the camp commandant was likewise pleased. If they were happy, we were happy - but only for so long.

The sapper cadets amongst us knew that we had experienced nothing yet. Gordon Barracks, the home of the Royal Engineers Officer Cadet School lay ahead. The stories we had heard about Mons had turned out to be true, but at least the discipline had not been of a 'bloody minded nature'. However, the tales that were told regarding Gordon Barracks were of a different nature and intensity; we had experienced nothing yet. This meant that none of us was in any way relishing the prospect of a three-month sojourn there - but it had to be undertaken if we wanted to try for a commission. Thus, two days after finishing at Mons we sappers were on our way to Gordon Barracks in Gillingham.

Before departing Aldershot we had one further task to carry out; we had to get a brown trilby hat for civilian wear at our next camp, which we had been informed was mandatory. A brown trilby hat together with our very light fawn coloured Macintoshes fairly singled us out as officer cadets. In Aldershot in particular, you had to be prepared for derogatory remarks, mainly from Teddy Boys. So, all kitted out, we set off for our next port of call. Here, I was fortunate because I was friendly with one of the RE cadets who possessed a car - wow, a car! So it was that I was able to get a lift to Gillingham, kit and all, and there was a lot of it, for the next venture into the unknown.

Royal Engineers Officer Cadet School, Gordon Barracks, Gillingham, Kent

We arrived at Gordon Barracks in Gillingham, which was close to the home of the Royal Engineers, which was based at Brompton Barracks in Chatham, just a few miles down the road. We arrived late in the afternoon of Wednesday 5 March 1958, just in time to un-pack all our kit and get ready for dinner in the officers mess at 6.30 p.m. A lounge suit was mandatory for dinner in the evening each night of the week. It was only on Saturday afternoon and all day Sunday that a sports jacket and flannels was permitted in the mess. Then it started, we were back to bulling our kit until 3.30 a.m. and this continued for many nights after our arrival. Naturally, this did not leave much time for sleep since reveille was at 6.00 am each day - Sunday excluded, when you could sleep as long as you wished - duties, exercises and studying permitting.

At this juncture it would help to clarify matters if I outlined the command structure at Gordon Barracks. The course here lasted three months and there was an intake each month of nominally 30-50 cadets. The Cadet Squadron was divided into three troops viz. Junior troop, Intermediate troop and Senior troop, with each intake progressing through the troops each successive month. The permanent staff members on the camp were senior army officers and NCOs who took responsibility for the training of the cadets, and of course, overseeing the whole camp. The senior cadet troop, under a few senior cadets, was allocated the responsibility for discipline within the cadet squadron, and therein lay the rub. These cadets had had nine or more months of, in army parlance, being f****d around from pillar to post: now was their time for payback, and the Junior Troop was always firmly in their sights. Inspections could be at any time during the day or night and it was because of that the Junior Troop often did not sleep in their beds for the first two weeks at least, lest there was a sudden inspection during the night. So, for the first two or three weeks we slept under our beds with the beds made up in immaculate fashion ready for the unexpected. And these inspections for room and kit, not just in the first week, but also throughout the course, were rigorous in the extreme. One soon found out that our dust had dust upon it, in places that dust should not be, even although we had already carried out our preparations most carefully. Punishment parade could be expected to follow; and did. Punishment parades at Gordon Barracks differed from most other camps. At Gordon Barracks, instead of parading in your best battle dress and best boots for the parade, here, you could wear anything you desired, from pyjamas to 'tinkers mufti', but always with the proviso that you wore some form of headgear, which could be anything of your choosing. Naturally, those on punishment parade did their best to appear before the senior cadet with the most outrageous apparel that they could think of. But it was never a good idea to be on punishment parade if it could be avoided. At Gordon Barracks the three-month course was intense with barely time for sleep, never mind any extra duties dished out by the senior cadet. Once you got behind on any aspect of the work it got more and more difficult to catch up, and catch up you must, otherwise you would be returned to your unit as a sapper in double quick time. Cadets could also be returned to their unit for failing the weekly exams, or for failing to perform to a satisfactory standard in any aspect of the training. On occasions, a cadet could be 'back squadded' for a month if, for example, he fell ill and was not able to undertake some part of the training. This allowed the cadet to recover from the ailment and re-join the next troop as they moved up the pecking order. I think it was the case that it was not normal to allow anyone to be 'back squadded' by more than one month because of the fact that it was considered that the time you would have as a commissioned officer would not be worth the time and money expended on training.

Some time shortly after arriving at Gordon Barracks the Senior Troop always had their Commissioning Parade. On the evening before the parade it was customary for the senior cadets to have a dance. Naturally, it fell to the Junior Troop to help with the preparations for the dance, in their own time [sic], and then after the dance was finished - usually about midnight - the Junior Troop then had to do the clearing up and get everything back to being 'tickety boo'. But it was never that straightforward. Due to the Commissioning Parade being the next day, by the time we had cleared up early that morning, we then had to have a kit inspection prior to the parade. In our case, that took place at 2.30 a.m. that morning. By the time the Senior Cadet was satisfied with our turnout it was time for some kip - well until reveille at 6.00 a.m.

For the duration of our three months at Gordon Barracks we carried out all the training expected of a sapper, and sapper officer, but to a considerably higher standard than before. For example, we were taught how to design Bailey Bridges, and then we would be tasked with organising and assembling all the necessary parts, including the transport, to build such a bridge over a designated obstacle. Thereafter, we would have a night exercise to build our bridge. Heaven help you if you had forgotten to order some part of the kit, which meant that after arriving at your destination you found that the bridge could not be built because some pin or other had been left behind, or not ordered. It was then that you realised that your prospects of progressing on the course had all but vanished. If all was progressing well then it was usually time for Sod to re-appear. The supervising officer or NCO would then decide that things were too easy and that Bailey bridge panels that had normally been six man loads for sappers were immediately designated to be four man loads for cadets. You soon found out that as a potential sapper officer you had to go the extra mile. Some cadets suffered from this in later life with back problems. The training exercise for this part of the course, known as *Quo Vadis*, took place when we were in the Intermediate Troop. We started work first thing in the morning and then worked all day and night grabbing what sleep you could, weather and time permitting. The ideal situation was to be able to finish the exercise and get back to camp before reveille in order that we could barge in and turf the Junior Troop out of their beds and mess up their kit - just for the hell of it. They were never very pleased about that since it meant that the Senior Troop would descend on them and demand some hurried inspections. Oh, the joys!

Then there was watermanship. At No. 3TRRE we had been restricted to rafts and pontoons and other floating equipment that was suitable for Hawley Lake, which was our training area. Now we were close to the tidal river of the Medway and there were no restrictions to the size of floating equipment that could be assembled. Heavy Ferries were great fun. They were nothing more that a very large and heavy metal pontoon powered by what looked like a jet engine in each corner of the ferry. These engines could generate an enormous thrust, which meant that a fair bit of speed could be reached on the river. With an engine in each corner of the pontoon they were also fairly manoeuvrable. Thus we were able to transport TCVs across the Medway. Initially, the supervising staff took great care to ensure that no other shipping was plying its trade on the river at that time. Once some degree of competence had been achieved we were allowed to have a few night schemes on the river, and take full responsibility for obeying the rules of the river. It was on one such exercise that to our great consternation we managed to collide with a Royal Navy ship. None of us cadets knew whether it was a frigate or destroyer or whatever, it was just a large vessel that to our mind had got in our way. The damage to the Heavy Ferry was non-existent, but to the navy vessel there were some very minor scratches - at least as far as we could tell in the darkness. It was decidedly scary and we all felt that we were soon going to be for 'the plank' - but surprisingly little was said. We later learned that the commander of the frigate, or whatever it was, had been court-martialled. A court martial did not mean that the commander was in the wrong, but merely that proceedings had been started to arrive at some conclusion regarding the incident. The fact that we heard nothing further suggested to us rather shaken cadets that perhaps he had been found negligent in some way or other, otherwise we would have certainly suffered some form of retribution. Nevertheless, we all felt some guilt ourselves. But the real fun during the three months at Gordon Barracks was demolitions and booby trapping. This was, in the main, carried out at Upnor Hard, which was close by on the south bank of the River Medway. Upnor Hard for years had been one of the traditional training areas for the Royal Engineers. Here we were able to indulge ourselves in bangs of all types, big and small, but the big ones were the always best. 'Beehives' that could shoot through two inches of solid steel, and underground explosive charges to blow huge craters in the ground, sufficient to stop tanks in their tracks. These were great fun. Then there were the explosive 'necklaces' that could shear through thick steel members, 'Wombats' and 'Bangalore Torpedoes' to fire across minefields to clear a safe path, and 'Hayricks' for shearing steel bridge members - all hugely enjoyable.

However, the night exercises for this aspect of the training were not a barrel of laughs. These exercises meant crawling on your stomach through minefields disarming mines. And why was it always the case that it had been raining immediately prior to the exercise making the ground sodden and boggy? It meant a very uncomfortable day and night in soggy denims. My diary notes it was 3.45 a.m. before we completed the last of the night schemes with reveille at 6.00 a.m. Tempers could get more than a little frayed when sleep was in short supply.

But the best was yet to come - the HARP, or High Altitude Rocket Projectile. This was a bit of kit - a rocket obviously, that could be fired over a distance of half a mile or thereby carrying a light load. Normally this would be a harpoon shaped projectile attached to which was a considerable length of rope. This was then used to fire across ravines, rivers or other difficult obstacles, to enable a crossing and bridgehead to be established. It was spectacular to see these projectiles snaking skywards with a length of rope trailing behind. We were ever so grateful to 'Betty Windsor' for allowing us to partake of these pleasures. On these occasions it seemed that the army was not such a bad place after all.

In addition to the field engineering we had the normal lectures on military law, tactics and organisation carrying on from where we had left off at Mons. It goes without saying that we also had the mandatory exams in bridge design, basic structural engineering as applied to military situations, road design and the planning and organising for all sorts of military situations from kit, men, transport, food and all forms of logistics. The exams for these modules were weekly and you were expected to pass every time. If I remember correctly, you were allowed one failure in one exam in each of Junior, Intermediate and Senior Troops, but you had to pass the one and only re-sit each time, otherwise you were 'out the door'. Occasionally a cadet, or cadets, would disappear from the troop for this very reason.

Each week it was the case that one cadet would be appointed class senior and was responsible for the turnout of the troop and most things associated with it for that week. It meant that, in addition to your own workload, you had to be keeping an eye on the others to ensure that everything was going to plan and that there were not going to be any 'black marks' coming your way. It was the case that on one of the occasions that I was class senior we had a big parade on the Sunday in Rochester. That particular week my letters home shows that we had two long reports to write up (amongst the many) and a multitude of other tasks to complete. With the added responsibility of ensuring that our troop was up to scratch for the parade it was the case that one just had to get the head down and get on with it - the time for moaning was later - much later. Fortunately, by this stage of training we were in the Intermediate Troop, which meant that the Senior Troop had their eyes more firmly aligned to the Junior Troop than to our troop. We did appear to have rather a lot of parades, not all of which I can recollect, but from my diaries it was the case that we had another big parade on Sunday 23 April 1958, which was a Memorial Service for the Royal Engineers held in Rochester Cathedral. This necessitated a two-mile march through Chatham to the cathedral in the centre of Rochester, in front of some very 'top brass'. Fortunately, the weather was not too hot and all went off very well. But these parades were never kind to your best kit, with the result that after such a parade you were left with a lot more 'bulling' to do just to get your kit back up to scratch again. You could never win.

And then there was Captain D; who could ever forget Captain D? He was a big, well built RE officer, of either American or Canadian nationality. He was always bright and alert and would never tire of exhorting you to give of your very best. He was not a man to accept anything less than a one hundred per cent effort.

His famous catch phrase was *grab your tutti frutties and Hersey bars and lets move.* To be under the vigilant eye of Captain D you had to be energised, enthusiastic and engaged with the task in hand; or, as he was often to remark, *bright eyed and bushy tailed.* He accepted nothing less than your very very best. Nevertheless, he was a great character and got the absolute maximum out of each and every one of us cadets, but it was bloody hard graft.

But all was not doom and gloom. It was normally the case that all stops would be pulled out during the week to try and have some free time at the weekend - duties permitting. On one rather delightful weekend I managed to travel to Canterbury with another of the cadets - Derek J - the cadet who had given me a lift from Mons to Gordon Barracks and who was a graduate art student from Blackpool. It was not a long visit but we managed to have a tour of the cathedral - which was magnificent - and then tea in the quaintly named Queen Elizabeth Guest Chambers, which was a tearoom. We convinced ourselves we deserved it. Such small pleasures lifted the spirits no end. And on another occasion Derek and I managed a Saturday trip to London, there to see the musical *Free As Air* at the Savoy Theatre in the Strand. The theatre will no doubt have changed considerably due to the fact that it was more or less rebuilt following a fire in the very early 1990s. Afterwards, we had a meal in a German restaurant in Soho. We did appear to 'live it up'. Perhaps the thought that we may just get our commissions was going to our heads.

In early April we had a few days leave for some reason or another. Whatever the reason it was all very welcome, although I did not get any more sleep at home than I had in the barracks - with so little free time, it could not be wasted. Towards the end of May 1958 we had some Whitsun leave, which was also very welcome; from last parade Friday 23 May to first parade Tuesday 27 May. As was normally the case when I was at Gordon Barracks I could never get to Kings Cross in time for the 4.00 p.m. Talisman express train. Consequently, it was the next available train, which, as I have already mentioned, did not get into Edinburgh Waverley until 3.43 a.m. on the Saturday morning. With departure being on the Monday evening, it did not leave a lot of time to enjoy the leave, particularly when it was an opportunity to catch up on some 'shut eye'. As was normal with British Rail, the trains were never very punctual; particularly it seemed, on the trains travelling south. So, on the return journey to camp after arriving at Kings Cross I would travel across London to Charing Cross Station and more often than not I would miss my connection to Gillingham. So it was a case of waiting at Charing Cross from 2.15 a.m. until 4.15 a.m. to get the milk train, which was never a fast express at the best of times. Unfortunately, at these unearthly hours everything was locked up so there was no warming 'cuppa' to while away the hours. Consequently, it was not until 7.00 a.m. that I could get to Gordon Barracks - just in time to get ready for first parade. To miss that would have been a very black mark indeed. Naturally, having missed a days training because of the leave, it was 'catch up time', and much was the midnight oil that was burned to complete our many duties and reports. I usually managed to get to bed by about 3.00 a.m. for the reminder of that week, but some poor sods were often up until 5.00 a.m. We sometimes wondered if it was worth it, but by now were nearly at the end of our officer cadet training and to wilt now would have been a complete waste of the previous nine months. We were not going to slip up now; if anything, it was time to 'dig deep' and make sure we did not falter in the last few weeks. As the then Winston Churchill would mutter to his acolytes in times of stress - *KBO* (*keep buggering on*).

By the time we were ending our period in Senior Troop were starting to make our choices about where we would like to be posted - assuming we got commissioned. There were a number of choices given to us; from Hong Kong, Singapore, Germany and the UK. Christmas Island was another posting, although I'm not sure that was on offer when we were told the available choices. There were only a few places available for the choice postings of Hong Kong and Singapore. Would we be lucky we wondered? No chance! Three of our cadets had, sometime early in their time at Gordon Barracks, indicated that they would enlist for a short service commission, so it was no surprise to find out that by the greatest of good luck they had managed to secure the only three places available for the choice postings. My second choice was the UK, as I did not particularly fancy Germany, which was reputed to be boring in the extreme. The upside of Germany was that the barracks were generally of a much higher standard than those in the UK. That was certainly no surprise! I was lucky, I was told that I was getting my second choice of posting which was the UK, and that I would be posted back to 3TRRE in Training Brigade, where I had done my basic training. Coincidentally, Rusty was to be the other cadet that was being posted to 3TRRE with me. It was only when in Senior Troop that I became friendly with Rusty. Rusty was Indian, but a fully naturalised British citizen who had been to public school in England. A public school that was renowned for producing talented sportsmen and senior army personnel. He had originally been destined for the University of Cambridge, but his father died when in his last year at school, so finances made that impossible. Immediately prior to joining our Senior Troop, Rusty had been in a state of limbo for a month having been back-squadded because of the fact that he had injured his left hand collar bone playing rugby for the regiment. So, when his injury had healed sufficiently, he joined us in Senior Troop. It was also around this time that we received our dress uniform (Blues), although I do not remember if we were issued with them or had to buy them. But the particular delight at this time was going up to Bond Street to purchase our service dress caps from the famed military hatters - Herbert Johnson. Surely, we thought, they wouldn't have allowed us to acquire these items if we weren't going to be commissioned.

But first, there were still some days to go and 'there's many a slip twixt cup and lip'. Now was the time to keep one's focus. On the last weekend in May and the first in June I spent the weekend assisting [sic] the orderly officer at Gordon Barracks. By now we were well into being 'commission happy'. Friday 30 May 1958 saw us cadets in the Senior Troop put on the obligatory cabaret at the Senior Troop Dance, a function that I just cannot recollect; so I have no idea what we did for the cabaret. Sunday 1 June was our commissioning service in the Garrison Church and then on Tuesday 3 June we had our Commissioning Parade at Brompton Barracks which just a few miles from our base at Gordon Barracks.

Brompton Barracks was the home of the Royal Engineers and an altogether more up-market establishment than the wooden spiders that we occupied at Gillingham. It was a rather elaborate and palatial place with a sumptuous mess; clearly a fitting home for a Corps headquarters. Even the parade ground was much more elaborate with a marble arched pillared entrance to it, rather reminiscent of Marble Arch in London. Unfortunately, the weather that day was not at its best - a 'smirring' of rain and a bit wet; but who cared, we had made it, and it all went off rather well. It was only when doing my research for this book that I discovered that we cadets had been listed in the London Gazette as being commissioned on Saturday 28 May, a week before the Commissioning Parade. If we had known that at the time we could have relaxed that bit earlier - but perhaps they had been wise to keep it from us for we still had a few exams in that final week and some other tasks to be carried out - all to the satisfaction of the supervisors. With the commissioning parade and all other duties over, it was time to say farewell to our colleagues. Team mates who had helped through thick and thin and who were departing for destinations unknown. It was likely we would never meet again.

But for now, it was time for some well earned leave - 10 glorious days lay ahead. And glorious they were, during which time Lorna and I got engaged. Of course the downside to all this was that one had to go back to camp at the end of the ten days. This was never an easy or pleasant time in the leave, and on this particular leave it was decidedly 'gut wrenching'. But it had to be done; so on Saturday 14 June 1958 I had to leave Edinburgh on the late evening train and travel back overnight to Kings Cross. True to form, the train was late in arriving, which on this particular occasion, was fortuitous. It meant that instead of arriving at Kings Cross at 7.30 a.m. the train arrived at 8.30 a.m. - less time to kill in London. So, after depositing all my kit in the left luggage office, I was able to have a walk around London taking in the sights since my train to Farnborough was not due to depart Waterloo until 3.00 p.m. that afternoon. This gave me time to have a wash and shave in the station before setting out on my tourist walking tour. The weather was good, the city was quiet and it was all rather lovely. Eventually, after a quite lengthy walk, I ended up on the South Bank where I was able to pen a few lines home and get them posted in time to catch the Sunday mail collection at noon - such a thing did exist in those days. Then, at 3.00 p.m., I departed on the train from Waterloo Station for Farnborough, and onwards to Guillemont Barracks near Cove.

3TRRE, Guillemont Barracks, Cove, Hampshire

Since this was my first time back at the camp as a subaltern I was making sure that I arrived in good time for the first parade on Monday, and that British Rail would not get me a 'black mark' for a late arrival. When I arrived at No. 3TRRE on the Sunday evening and having reported to the Officers' Mess I found out that I was allocated to share a room with Rusty until such time as some single accommodation became available. He was already ensconced in the billet when I arrived. The sleeping quarters for the officers that lived on camp was essentially the same construction as the spiders for the sappers, except that they did not have a spider layout, and the rooms were in the main single rooms with the occasional double room. This suited Rusty and I very well. As new subalterns it meant we could easily exchange notes each evening and roundly curse the army to our hearts content - if we so desired, and we often did. We also had been told that we would share the services of a civilian batman. It turned out that he was Welsh, of late middle age, and the secretary of the local communist party and more than a little prickly tempered. 'Taff' was certainly the most unlikely person to have as a batman in the officers' mess and was happy to make known his displeasure at having the job, if given half a chance. Why he had ever applied for the post we never found out. Bright and early on the Monday morning Rusty and I presented ourselves to the camp Adjutant - Captain John G - at the appointed hour and duly introduced ourselves. After the usual introductory lecture we were told what our duties were to be. Rusty was being allocated to 'C' Squadron, which was the administration squadron in charge of the day to day running of the camp, from the cookhouse to the military transport wing, and all the duties related to life on the camp. I was allocated to 'B' Squadron which was one of the two training squadrons charged with training new recruits in infantry skills and basic military engineering; the other squadron carrying out the same tasks was 'A' Squadron. Rusty and I then made our separate ways to report to our respective OCs in charge of the squadrons. In my case this was a Major ?, whose name I have forgotten. After reporting to the squadron office I had a long and apprehensive wait before seeing the OC as he was already occupied in a meeting. As it so happened there had been nothing to be apprehensive about - he was very welcoming and it seemed to me that he would be a good officer to serve under. I was told that I was going to replace second lieutenant Dick C, who was due to be demobbed in two weeks time. That seemed to me to be an ideal situation; I would have two weeks to get acquainted with his NCOs and Party before he departed. And so I made my way to the squadron lines and to the troop office to meet Dick C. By this time it was late into the afternoon because our first meeting with the adjutant had not been able to take place until quite late in the morning because of his prior commitments. As luck would have it Dick C was in the troop office as was Cpl M, who was the acting party sergeant at the time. After the usual introductions Dick happily informed me that he was going to be demobbed in two weeks time and still had some leave due to him. Now that I had arrived he was going to take some of his leave now. *Chic here are the keys of the troop office, I'll leave you and Cpl M to get on with it. I'll be back in 72 hours.* And so he departed. Not quite what I had been anticipating. So, I had my chat with Cpl M to assess the situation and decide what we were going to do. The troop, he told me, were out in the training area doing some field engineering and already had duties allocated for that evening. By now it was late afternoon and that suited me just fine. *OK.* I said, *there's nothing I can usefully do today so I'm going back to the mess to get all my kit un-packed and ready for life at No. 3. I'll meet up with the other NCOs before first parade tomorrow and then introduce myself to the troop.* That suited us both. I then told him my room number in the mess, as was customary, in case there was any emergency that needed my immediate attention. This room number was, by default, also recorded in the Guard Room. So, I returned to my room to do my un-packing, have my evening meal in the mess, and then get an early night because I had not wasted much time on my leave on sleep. Things were looking good, or so I thought… But I had been rather hasty in arriving at that conclusion.

Somewhere between 2.00 a.m. and 3.00 a.m. there was a very loud and urgent banging on the door. "Mr Husband, the Guard Commander needs you in the guard room PDQ". Bloody hell thought I, what could necessitate him wanting me at this hour. Rusty merely cursed loudly, turned over and went back to sleep. After hastily getting dressed I duly reported to the guardroom. It was then that the corporal of the guard told me that a sapper in our/my troop had tried to commit suicide and that I was needed in the spider ASAP. He was not wrong. Sapper X, it turned out, had tried to shoot himself but had only been saved from succeeding by the sapper in the next bed being awakened by his efforts and managing to restrain him until the room corporal arrived on the scene. By the time I got there the situation was in a reasonable state of control, but clearly, every one in the room was very shaken by the proceedings. One of the things that Her Majesty did not appreciate was soldiers trying to take their own life, so there was nothing for it, I had to put Sapper X. on a charge and have him marched to the Detention Centre under close arrest. For some reason Provo. Sergeant H was on duty - a task that would have normally fallen to one of his corporals. He was not at all pleased to have been awakened from his slumbers at that un-earthly hour. After explaining the situation I then had to get the Provo. Sergeant to arrange hourly watches on the sapper to ensure that he did not make another attempt on his life. That was an unlikely scenario because as soon as you were admitted to 'The Block' (Detention Centre) you were stripped of all webbing and anything else that could assist in a suicide attempt, or an attack on the guards. Even your eating irons were kept out-with the cell which was sparsely furnished to say the least. In the morning I then had to get the Medical Officer to check the sapper and take responsibility for his immediate future. Returning to the spider I soon found the room corporal was slowly returning the situation to normal. This was not the introduction to the troop that I had planned. I confiscated the Lee Enfield that sapper X had used and the .303 cartridge that he had attempted to use in his failed attempt. The round that he had used had miss-fired. He had made three attempts to fire his rifle and on each occasion the cartridge had not ignited because, as I discovered, there were three indentations in the base of the cartridge, one for each missfire. It was Sapper X's lucky day, although he would not have appreciated that at the time. The initial mystery was where had he got the .303 round? Security on camp was tight, and on the rifle ranges it was extremely tight. All ammunition was kept under secure lock and key and all rounds had to be fired, or accounted for. An investigation then revealed that he had found an unexpended cartridge when the troop were firing on the rifle ranges and kept it for his unsavoury task. Finding live rounds on the rifle ranges was not an uncommon event. The ranges had been used for training purposes before, during and after WWII and unexpended rounds were everywhere. Valiant efforts had been made at various times to clear the ranges of these rounds, but inevitably, not every round could be found, hidden as they were in tufts of grass and undergrowth. Sapper X had found one such round and instead of reporting it and handing it in to the NCO in charge, he had kept it for his suicide attempt. Clearly, he had planned ahead. But Sapper X had made one mistake. These were very old rounds that could be found on the ranges, and consequently unreliable. He had made the mistake of not substituting the round he had found for one of the new live rounds that he would have been given for his rifle practice. He could have used the old round during his rifle practice and if it had misfired, he would have been given another round in lieu - a mistake that was to save his life. The next day, after an examination by the Medical Officer, Sapper X was transferred to Cambridge Military Hospital for assessment and possible treatment. After that we were never informed of what had happened to him. All in all, it had been a more eventful start to life at 3TRRE than what I had been anticipating.

Because I was 2IC to second lieutenant Dick C for the two weeks until he was demobbed I had some surplus time on my hands, so one day I found myself invigilating officer at a GCE examination for military personnel that was being held in Aldershot. The subject was music. Clearly, it was not a popular subject in the Aldershot Garrison Area because there was only one candidate taking the examination; but at least it made for a good afternoon's skive.

We also had on our camp a cadre for trainee NCOs. This cadre lasted two weeks before they were posted for more specialist training. If they passed the course they then became potential

NCOs. Without question, this cadre turned out a very well presented troop. As I had just arrived at the camp and the cadre troop were near to completion of their two week course I found myself being the examining officer in all aspects of their field engineering. As I recollect, they all passed with flying colours. Of course, once it became known that you were available to carry out some extra-mural duties it was not long before some of the other subalterns started to try to offload their workload, or at least those parts of it that they preferred to dodge. So it was that one day I found myself taking a troop of sappers up to London to show them the delights of the Imperial War Museum. They had obviously seen enough of the army already because their boredom was very obvious. However, they were all enjoying the fact that it was a day away from their 'Lance Jacks' and the constant shouting and swearing. Into the bargain, their troop officer had decreed that they could have the evening free in London before returning to camp. This free evening enabled me to meet up with Ken R who had been with me in basic training at 3TRRE back in October, November and December. Because he had been a solicitor in civilian life he had managed to get transferred to the army legal branch, and been made up to sergeant without any of the hassle of intermediate training that we had gone through. And the posting, being based in London, as it so happened, was the icing on the cake. As might be imagined London was a cushy posting. Lucky blighter! It was only a short meeting as I still had the troop of sappers to oversee, but we were able to make arrangements to meet up at a later date, at a time when I would not have other responsibilities to attend to.

These few trips were the benefits of being 2IC for a short while, but soon I was fully immersed in the work of the party. Tasks such as taking the night schemes and other more bothersome duties that Dick felt that he could well do without, being so near to demob as he was. That was fair enough! It was on one of those watermanship night schemes on Hawley Lake that two NCOs from one of the other parties in 'A' Squadron were drowned. It was a most unpleasant period and the fact that it had been at night made the rescue operation that much more difficult. Hawley Lake was a large lake, mainly surrounded by trees, and being situated well into the country, there was little or no light to aid in the search and rescue operation, making it a very difficult task. The rescue operation fell to the responsibility of the Duty, or Orderly Officer, as the troop officer was elsewhere on other duties. It was a harsh reality check for the regiment who endeavoured to maintain high standards at all times.

Dick C was now in 'wind down' time and so delegated his last night scheme to me. I remember not what we were doing, but just that it was the 'mother and father' of a thunderstorm all night and we got absolutely drenched - almost waterlogged. We were wiggling our toes in the lukewarm water in our boots. Dick was delighted he had made the right call.

Then, in early July 1958, our Commanding Officer was contacted by the police to give assistance in the search for a convict that had escaped from Broadmoor Mental Institution, which was only six miles or so from our camp. The convict in question turned out to be 'Mad Frank Mitchell' the 'Axe Man', a man of immense stature and strength, so named because the axe was his preferred weapon of choice with which to threaten or injure his victims. Early in his career he had been charged with attempted murder, but acquitted, and then later still, charged with attacking police officers with two meat cleavers. Altogether, he was a most undesirable companion, not to say adversary. It was thought that he might be hiding in the woods at Hartley Whitney, an area close by to 3TRRE. So our camp was requested to send out search parties to comb the likely spots where he might be hiding. This meant that we had to mobilise our troops into small groups to do the needful. Naturally, when it was explained to the sappers what we expected of them they were not too amused -

neither were the troop officers who were going to be leading the search teams.

Consequently, we were bussed, courtesy of the police, to the targeted woods, nooks and crannies that were possible hiding places and asked to get on with it, under their supervision. The use of weapons was taboo for such an operation and so the only thing that the sappers could be equipped with was pick helves (i.e. pick handles). But there were not enough to go around, so only every third or fourth sapper could be so equipped. Those without such a defence weapon, including the troop officers, clearly felt rather naked when there was the possibility that they might have to tackle 'Mad Frank Mitchell', the man that had garnered a reputation for his lack of civilities when confronted with folks that he did not care for. Oh the joys! As luck would have it he had already made himself scarce some time before we arrived, if he had ever been there at all. Soon after this he was arrested on a Bournemouth to London coach. Thankfully, the passengers on the bus were unaware of their nefarious travelling companion until the police intercepted the bus - mob handed. He was minus axe and meat cleavers at the time of arrest.

Later that month we had the Aldershot & District Athletics championships, which were held in Aldershot. This was another occasion when, not having a troop of my own at that stage, I was charged with organising the team transport and the assembly and dispersal of the team, for the two days of the championships. It was a particularly exciting competition which went 'down to the wire', with 3TRRE winning the overall trophy on the last event of the last day. Being a training regiment the CO could, if alerted, often have particularly talented sappers posted back to us, or retained within the permanent staff on our camp, to compete for us in various sports. So it was no surprise that 3TRRE was nearly always represented in the finals of the Army and Southern Command, rugby, football and athletics competitions. It was only when speaking with Rusty when I was doing my research for this book that I learned that our CO had arranged for Rusty to be posted back to Guillemont Barracks after he had been commissioned. This was because Rusty was an extremely talented rugby player and cricketer. He played rugby to the army team standard and was of minor counties standard at cricket. From memory, we also had two international footballers playing for us in the soccer team. One was Davie W of Glasgow Rangers and the other international player was English, but I confess that I have long forgotten his name. We also had an athletics track located a short distance from the Officers Mess and it was very common to see the sportsmen on the permanent staff training there on a regular basis, and always on a Wednesday afternoon.

Tuesday 15 July 1958 saw the 'Pass off Parade' for the troop that I had inherited from Dick C, as he had now long since been demobbed. As was the case the troop officer arranged for a trip to London the evening before pass off for the sappers to see a show and let their hair down for a few hours. The timing of this visit was particularly crazy, but it was the only time in the recruits' schedule that such an event could take place because, on the afternoon/evening after pass off, the recruits dispersed for some leave, and then onwards to their next posting. On this particular occasion they had expressed an interest in a show at the London Palladium, so that was what I organised for them. Everything went off well and all sappers duly appeared on the London Embankment at the appointed hour of 11.00 p.m. to be bussed back to camp for 'Pass off Parade' the next day. It was always a relief not to have lost a sapper on their last, and only, evenings 'piss up'.

With my first party gone I had about ten days before the next intake arrived, which meant that it gave some time to catch up on the various administrations tasks that had to be undertaken between intakes. It was in this quieter period that I was able to reflect on my own circumstances and take stock of my finances since Lorna and I had become engaged in early June. I knew my worldly wealth would not be great, which meant that it did not take long to assess my financial standing in the greater scheme of things. It amounted to the grand total of £12. Sometime later I read in one of my letters home that I had resolved to try and save £6 per month towards married life. I'm not sure that I ever achieved that goal. It was not a lot to show for a five-year apprenticeship as a 'professional gentlemen' [sic] and one and a half years serving 'Betty Windsor'. And Lorna had even less to her name. Hmmm! Our financial prospects looked decidedly bleak. But the good news was that Lorna had a one-week holiday due to her and was arranging to spend it with some family friends In London. Unfortunately, I still had my duties to undertake; nevertheless, I might manage up to the metropolis one evening and possibly all weekend during that week.

July was proving to be a good month. I again made contact with Ken R, my friend in London, whom I had met not many weeks before and I arranged to visit him on a Saturday in the 'Big Smoke'. It proved to be a most enjoyable trip because in the morning he had arranged for us to visit the House of Commons and the House of Lords, together with a quick trip to Westminster Abbey. In the afternoon, by a stroke of good luck, we were able to get two cancellation tickets to see the West End Musical - *My Fair Lady*, starring Rex Harrison, Julie Andrews and Stanley Holloway. The two balcony seats cost us 5/- each, but I don't have a note of the theatre where the performance took place. The show was excellent and many people were standing in the aisles just to see the musical. We had been extremely fortune in being able to get a seat. Later that night, before heading back for the 10.00 p.m. train to Farnborough, we had coffee in a little café in Soho. It was here that the owner proudly informed us that his café was opposite to the café where Tommy Steele had first performed. Clearly, we were meant to be impressed.

This leisurely introduction to my new life at 3TRRE meant that there was time to assimilate into the routine of the officers' mess, which was decidedly more pleasant than living in a spider with twenty to a room. A bonus was that Rusty and I got on extremely well; so sharing a room with him was no hardship. It was in this early period in the mess that, another of the subalterns in 'B' Squadron - John F - introduced me to classical music. This was something with which I had little acquaintance, as I was never musically minded. Even to this day my family are of the opinion that I am tone deaf. Jean Sibelius, the renowned Swedish composer, was one of John's favourite composers and to this day I still enjoy *Finlandia* and the *Karelia Suite*. These are no doubt low grade on the classical scale, but still enjoyable. Around this time another of the subalterns was due for imminent demob and so it fell to me to step into his shoes as the officer in charge of the officers' mess bar. This was another of those little tasks that the more senior subalterns were happy to offload. Nevertheless, I was quite happy to carry out this duty since it involved very little work, other than being responsible for the running of the bar and the associated finances. The day to day duties were carried out by a full corporal, which for him was a much more pleasant duty than humping Bailey Bridge panels around, or doing minefield training or whatever - the downside was that the hours were not so sociable with many late evenings, although there was a duty rota with another junior corporal. I happily signed for the bar and so relieved the departing subaltern of his responsibilities, thinking in my innocence, that he would have had everything 'ship shape and Bristol fashion'. It was only then that the senior corporal alerted me to the fact that it might be wise to do a complete audit of the bar stock so that we were fully aware of our current assets. Clearly, he had intuitions that all was not as it should be because the previous incumbent had made no efforts to assess the stock during his time in office. So, one quiet Sunday I closed the bar for a few hours - something that was normally unthinkable and unpopular - but it had to be done to allow us to quickly do our audit. The corporal's intuitions had been correct; we were down in stock with every single item in the bar. Wines and spirits were low, but not abnormally so because they were dispensed with fixed measures. But the beer stock was on a different planet altogether. We were down by barrels and barrels and barrels of beer. Quite how this had happened no one knew. But now was not the time for reflections on what might have happened, now was the time for action. I was going to be the mess bar officer for the foreseeable future until such time as I could off load the responsibility to some more junior subaltern. So, between the corporals and myself we devised a strategy whereby the corporals would give a few short measures for the wine and spirits sales, for a very short period of time to bring stocks back up to the proper level; but what to do about the beer? There was nothing for it but to be aggressive with the measures for the pints and blatantly keep them short to enable stocks to be built back up again. It was with some apprehension the corporals agreed, worried that they would be verbally abused for giving short measures. I had to reassure them that they were acting under my orders and I would answer to any senior officer that blew his top. As it so happened, no one seemed to notice that the measures were less generous than had previously been the case and the whole exercise of damage limitation passed of remarkably well - just too well as it turned out. Very many months later when there was the opportunity for me to offload the duty onto another subaltern I thought it prudent to carry out another audit in advance of handover leaving sufficient time to enable further corrective action to be taken should our stocks still be below par. I needn't have worried. The audit showed that the wines and spirits were just where they should be - but the beer - oh dear! We had so much surplus amber stuff that it was embarrassing. We could have had a squadron party with free beer for everyone. The incoming subaltern was agreeable to accept the surplus, happy in the knowledge that he would have no worries when his time came to hand over the bar to another incumbent. The corporals and I had some free pints that evening. Prior to this it had been my habit to only have half pints in the bar to keep my mess bill down, but that evening I had pints on the house and told the corporals that they could do likewise, provided that they remained sober and compos mentis. Cheers all round!

It was not long after Dick C got demobbed that I got my own party. This meant taking a sergeant and a few corporals to 1TRRE at Merebrook Camp near Malvern to collect the next intake. We journeyed up one day staying overnight in the mess at 1TRRE ready for an early morning start the next day with the sergeant, corporals and new party back to 3TRRE. Already at 1TRRE were two other officers and NCOs from 6 & 9TRRE respectively, also waiting to collect their recruits. This was a scene that I well recollected from my time there in basic training with the sergeants and NCOs 'getting a grip' on the new intakes and putting the fear of death into them. Transport was provided by 1TRRE to take us in TCVs to the station at Malvern. Thereafter, the army had organised a special train to take the complement of men and kit to Reading, I think it was, where we all had to disembark for another special train to take us to Farnborough. Farnborough had, I seem to recall, three stations - Ash Vale, North Camp and Farnborough Main Line. Which of the stations we arrived at I cannot remember except that it was Farnborough Main Line station that was used when going to Waterloo for a day in London or home on a spot of leave. Once the new intake were back in 3TRRE it was time to get down to work. Training schedules had to be organised and all sappers had to be seen and documented, battle-dresses checked for fit and adjusted by the camp tailor as required, and of course the mandatory haircut, which, as I seem to recollect, cost a shilling - five pence in today's currency, but a lot back then. And there was extra equipment to be handed out and signed for. The first few days were always very hectic for everyone as so much had to be done, and so quickly. And then it was onto the parade ground to knock them into something resembling soldiers; a task that the corporals took great pride in doing and seemed to enjoy. But during this early part of the recruits training it was also important to speak to them and get them to tell you of any problems that they may have; relationships, or financial, or otherwise. This was an important part of the troop officer's duties because an unhappy or troubled sapper would rarely make a good soldier.

Many recruits would come from 'civvy street' earning a modest or reasonably wage, and if they were married, would possibly have hire purchase agreements to service, or rents for the marital home to be paid. As the wage for a trainee soldier was only twenty-eight shillings per week this was never usually enough to maintain the financial outlays that the soldier had previously undertaken. So, it was often the case that I found myself writing, or communicating with the hire purchase companies that they had obligations to, to negotiate a reduced and very modest payment until such time as the sapper received a better wage to allow him to pay more per week, or per month. Many of these companies were initially extremely un-cooperative and wanted to play 'hard ball' all the way. It was only when they were told that 'Betty Windsor' was going to hold onto her young charges for another two years and that they had better start getting realistic about what they could expect from the sapper, that common sense prevailed. It was always the case that a satisfactory settlement could then be agreed.

As most of the first few weeks of basic training was spent 'bulling kit' or drilling on the parade ground - tasks mainly carried out by the NCOs, and something they were well up for - it gave me time to do all the administration work associated with the troop. In this respect I was extremely fortunate because I had inherited from Dick C an extremely good set of NCOs. Once the initial four weeks of 'square bashing' was over it was time to start introducing the other more technical aspects of field engineering. This covered mine warfare, demolitions, booby traps, bailey bridging and pontoon bridging, watermanship, including knots and lashes and the old chestnut of digging trenches, foxholes and observation posts. The night exercises digging these various types of trenches and then protecting them with barbed wire or Dannert Coils could be a decidedly uncomfortable, nay prickly task. It was clear on these exercises that we were working the sappers extremely hard. On one of the night schemes - *Hedgehog* - which was due to last between 36-48 hours, I arranged for the cookhouse to supply the main hot meal of the day out on the training area. This was sometime around 9.00 p.m. in the evening on that particular day - a day when it had been raining hard and without respite. When the sappers lined up to get their meal I happened to notice that one of the cookhouse staff was about to put the sapper's custard, which was the desert course, into the same mess tin as his main course. Immediately I dashed over to admonish the cook when the sapper intervened. *Aw Sir, it disnae matter. That's what ah asked fur. I'm just too totally f****d to eat two course. Ah don't care.* He had obviously given his all.

Once the more technical aspects of the training started it afforded the opportunity to see how the sappers were progressing, and to see if any of the potential NCOs and potential officers were showing the extra aptitude or leadership that would allow them to be considered for a visit to WOSB. However, before that decision could be taken, there was a long selection process to go through. As I have already indicated earlier it all started with an interview with the troop officer to assess more thoroughly their capabilities for their potential grading. Depending on the number of potential candidates in each category it could take quite a fair bit time to complete the process since the interviews would last about an hour for a potential officer, and about half to three quarters of an hour for an NCO. Of course, there were shortcuts that could be taken. If a candidate was clearly inadequate the interview could be terminated after a short period of time. If a candidate was outstanding likewise was the case, meaning that the majority of interviews lasted the full time to allow a complete assessment to be made. All the reports were then hand written out together with the troop officer's recommendations and passed to the OC for his interview and subsequent decision as to whether or not the candidate would be allowed to progress further. There were also many times that the candidate, potential officer or NCO, decided that they did not want to traverse that path to potential promotion. That was their choice and had to be respected. Each candidate was made fully aware of the hard road that lay ahead if they decided to proceed. Any candidate with less than one hundred per cent commitment was doomed to an early failure. So, it was well into their training before the OC was able to make his recommendation as to their future prospects. With the NCOs this was the last hurdle in the selection process, but for the potential officers they still had to have their interview with the CO, assuming they were being allowed to progress that far.

During the technical aspects of the field engineering training we would hold examinations every week for all the sappers. These exams were, in the main, of a more practical nature. But each sapper had to satisfy the troop officer that he was sufficiently competent in his skills before he would be allowed to progress to the next part of training. A lack of competence meant that the sapper would be 'back squadded' to the more junior party following, to allow him more time to brush up on his skills. No sapper ever relished being 'back squadded'.

Meanwhile, settling into life in the officers' mess was good and whilst the food was not spectacular, it was still very satisfactory - particularly the curries for which our mess sergeant was renowned. This was the first time I had every had curry and I was particularly taken by it. From memory I think it was usually served once per week on a Tuesday evening and I always had curry on that night. As was usual in an officers' mess one night per week was 'blues night' when everyone was expected to attend and dress in their blues uniform. As was the custom on these nights the junior subaltern was tasked with giving the toast to the Queen before the meal started. There was a selection of standard toasts for such events, so the task was not onerous. This meant that the evening always started off very formally, but as the night progressed things could get decidedly frantic as the junior officers indulged in various mess games; which invariably ended in a rough and tumble. The one surprise was that no one was injured.

The only fly in the ointment was that any breakages had to be paid for by the participants. One night per month the CO would invite a guest, or guests, to attend one of these Thursday evenings 'blues night'. This was always a much more formal occasion and all the officers, without question, were expected to stay for the whole evening until the last of the guests had departed. This could sometimes be very fraught for the subalterns who had to be on an early morning parade or duty, particularly if the guests did not depart until the early hours. It was not unknown for them to stay until 3.00 a.m. or later.

It was on one such evening some many months after I had joined the mess that we had a particularly boring 'mess night' with the guests lingering on well into the 'wee sma hours'. As it so happened the following day several of us junior officers had a 6.00 a.m. start to the day. As the night crept on we realised that we were going to get very little sleep - if any at all. So it was that we decided that one by one each of us would slip away surreptitiously in the hope that no one would notice our non-attendance - particularly the senior ranks who were all very ensconced with each other. But we were wrong. The 2IC of the regiment had noticed, or had brought to his notice, that a few of the junior members of the mess were missing. Consequently, sometime on the following day our small group were summoned to his office and given a dressing down which ended up with each of us being given extra orderly officers duties - eleven each as I seem to recall. This was not a particularly welcome outcome as it meant another eleven 24-hour days with the consequent paucity of 'shut eye'. Fortunately, we were able between us to arrange to stagger these duties to avoid having eleven 24-hour duties on the trot, although that had not been what the 2IC had in mind when he meted out the punishments. In addition to the extra duties we were given some early morning parades at 6.30 a.m. These were under the watchful eye of the RSM. A task that I think he felt he could well have done without. It was on these parades that we junior subalterns had to each take it in turn to drill the squad with various drill routines. It was all a bit of a bore, but when the RSM was out of earshot the subaltern commanding the squad at that particular time would start to shout out his commands in cryptic terms. *Oranges and Lemons* and other nonsensical non-military terms were used. The result was that the squad would end up in total disarray not understanding what the command meant. Thus, it gave the 'subbie' in charge a chance to shout abuse at his charges, all of course, in diplomatic language befitting a junior officer. Naturally, this alerted the RSM to the goings on so he would start to take a keen interest again. It was good fun, but self-defeating as it merely prolonged the drill parades. With regard to the duty officers duties, these started when the nominal working day had ended e.g. 6.00 p.m. At that time - when there was no IRA alert - you then had to parade in your blues uniform, with sword, to inspect the guard at the guard room, and then undertake a series of checks around the camp before snatching a quick meal in the mess. After that it was another series of checks and inspections around the camp, including the guard platoon itself, before a quick kip around midnight - assuming there had been no untoward event that had required your attention. Then, usually about 1.00 a.m. or thereby there would be another foot tour around the camp followed by a visit to the secure compound that nestled in the woods some distance from the camp. It was here that was stored the ammunition and explosives and some weapons that we used for our daily training and exercises. As I have said earlier, it was reputed that we had the largest store of explosives in Southern Command, something that was perfectly believable. Into this solid brick building, which was partially sunk into the ground, the guards on duty were locked in the building until the following day. There were no trainees in this guard; they were all experienced sappers or NCOS with specialist training in handling explosives. For the visit to the explosives compound in the winter we usually commandeered a driver and a 'Champ' vehicle (which as I seem to remember was a particularly unreliable set of 'wheels') to take us to a pre-arranged meeting at the compound with the dog patrol. The usual arrangement was to meet at irregular times and meeting points, at least twice during the night, to check the compound. The 'Champ' was normally parked some distance from the meeting point and the orderly officer would proceed on foot to meet the dog patrol. In the summer it was the same procedure, but I often cycled to the meeting points. The *normal* army dog team was a handler and a 'guard dog'; a four legged friend that had about six-eight weeks training, and was responsive to experienced handlers. Our dog patrols consisted of a handler and a 'war dog' that had only had about two-three weeks training, and was a particularly vicious brute that would only respond to its own handler. When you met with the patrol you had to keep at least five or six metres distant from the patrol, otherwise the dog was likely to try and attack you. After the check of the compound had been completed the duty officer would then be driven to the dog compound to check all was well. This compound was about a mile or more from the camp and situated on the edge of Hawley Lake close by to where Bailey bridging and watermanship training and exercises were carried out. By the time one had carried out two of these inspections during the night and toured the camp, and checked on the guard in the guardhouse, it left little time for 'shut eye' before your normal duties started early the next day. And all that assumed that nothing untoward had arisen during the night.

However, when we were on alert at times of heightened IRA activity, or anticipated activity, we would dress in our normal battle dress and carry a pistol. Such was the 'red tape' that had to be observed when carrying a pistol that it was generally felt that it was most useful as an implement that one could throw at the enemy rather than shoot at him. This was because the live rounds for the pistol had to be carried in a little box, rather like a matchbox, and it was sealed with tape. Consequently, it would have taken a good few minutes to have unsealed the box and loaded the firearm before it could be used. But even then you were not done. Next, we carried a little yellow card, which had to be extracted from the pocket, and the short written warning on the card had to be read to the potential target before the weapon could be fired. Yes, throwing the pistol at the target, or holding it by the barrel and using it as a striking implement had a lot of merit.

There was one other hazard of doing orderly officer duty in times of 'Low Alert' which a young subaltern had to be very aware of. It lay in the disguise of the duty sergeant. After all the official tasks had been carried out and there was a brief respite before it all started over again the sergeant and officer would disperse to their respective messes for a 'cuppa' or a brief 'kip'. If, and only if, you were on very good terms with the sergeant, or he thought you had 'made the grade', then on occasions, you might be invited into the sergeants' mess for a quick drink. At this juncture your antenna had to move into full alert made. Whilst the gesture was genuine, it was also a chance to try and get the young officer more than a little tipsy. The first line of defence was to have a very good excuse ready to decline the invitation should one be proffered, but an excuse that would not cause offence. If however, such an excuse did not fall readily to hand, or had been used on an earlier occasion then will power had to be used. Refuse all alcoholic drinks and stick to less harmful liquids, no matter what enticements or ridicule he might attempt. The more you could resist the enticements the more that he would respect you. And so you could excuse yourself after a decent interval of time and a few tales 'under the belt'. The sergeants' mess was always good for rumours that we in the officers' mess never got to hear about.

Nontheless, doing duty officer on occasions had its merits. At holiday weekends such as Whitsun, or other times when the holidays didn't exactly coincide with the Scottish holiday times, I could volunteer to be duty officer for the weekend and then take my few days break at another more convenient time. And it was often the case that Rusty did likewise for other reasons. And so we were often the duty officers in camp when the rest were on a short leave break. It was on one of these weekends that Rusty and I were duty officers that Rusty's OC, a bachelor who had a pet Labrador named 'Ricki' - that had a mind of its own - asked Rusty if he would look after 'Ricki' for a few days as he was taking the weekend leave. Naturally, Rusty felt obliged to do so. However 'Ricki' had his own plans and proved rather a handful over the weekend. I found that out when Rusty was doing his orderly officer stint and I was left with 'Ricki'. After a short spell with me 'Ricki' decided that he had had enough and made his bolt for freedom out of the camp into the 'wide blue yonder'. Now one of the rules for duty officers was that they were not allowed to leave camp during their spell of duty, consequently, Rusty and myself had to take it in turns to search for him out of camp - but it was all to no avail. So we could do nothing more than report 'Ricki's' disappearance to the local constabulary before Rusty's OC returned from his long weekend leave. Luck was on our side and soon 'Ricki' was returned to us in the back of some smart police vehicle. After duly thanking 'the boys in blue' Rusty and I decided that enough was enough. So I took 'Ricki', on a stout leash, to the camp detention centre, aka 'The Block'. Being a long holiday weekend there was only a corporal and a regimental policeman on duty since there were no detainees in the cells. Just the job I thought. So after a bit of chat I got the corporal to take 'Ricki' into the detention centre and provide him with his own cell. The plan being that we would retrieve 'Ricki' early on the Tuesday morning before everyone returned from leave. All appeared to go well until very early on the Tuesday morning when I got a message from Provo. Sergeant H who had also returned from leave, asking if I could come to the Detention Centre to see him. I duly did, and it was then I was confronted with 'Ricki' and the frustration of his enforced detention in the cell. The scene was one of utter devastation. 'Ricki' had gone berserk and destroyed just about everything that could be destroyed, and as for the mattress - well it was no longer discernible as such - it had been shredded into a thousand pieces. Naturally, the Provo. Sergeant was a bit put out, all the more so since he was now minus kit for the cell, which he had signed for 'many moons' previously. So, I agreed with Sergeant H that he would arrange for his men to clear up the cell and dispose of the debris and I would go to see the Quartermaster and sweet talk him into getting replacements for the damaged bedding and cabinet that 'Ricki' had so effectively decommissioned. After a bit of chitchat I was able to get the extra kit that was required, but only on the understanding that I would sign for it, since the Quartermaster had to be able to account for every item in the stores - particularly when the annual GOC's inspection took place. Thus, Sergeant H was mollified, the quartermaster was satisfied, and 'Ricki' was returned safely to his master without Rusty's OC being any the wiser. To this day the army will find that I still have a mattress, some bed linen and a bedside cabinet signed out in my name as no one had thought to check that on demob a young subaltern would have had such additional items signed out to him. Rusty duly made sure that on later weekends that he always had a good excuse to hand should he ever again be asked to look after the OC's beloved 'Ricki'.

On another occasion when I was duty officer early in December 1958 there was a rather more serious situation that arose. At this juncture it is necessary to say the we had a fairly new regimental sergeant major arrive on camp; one who was so Scottish that his accent was more than difficult to understand. I could make him out with some difficulty, but others who were not familiar with his broad accent had great difficulty in understanding him. So it was that he would often chat to me merely because I was one of the few officers that could hold a conversation with him, and we got on moderately well, although he was not an easy character to deal with. So much so that he had previously had trouble in his earlier career, serious enough that he had been reduced to the ranks. So it was to his credit that he had made it back to Regimental Sergeant Major. What these troubles had been I never found out, but in addition to them he had had previous convictions for attempting to beat his wife. So, it was on this particular night when I was duty officer, and long after I had completed my rounds and was getting 'a bit of kip' that there was a loud banging on the door of the room that I was sharing with Rusty. *Mr Husband, Mr Husband, the duty sergeant needs to see you in the guardroom PDQ.* So I got dressed and rushed up to the guardroom as fast as I could. There, I was confronted once more by 'the boys in blue'. Our beloved Regimental Sergeant Major, who lived in married quarters out of camp, was apparently trying to murder his wife, who, to protect herself, had locked herself in some storage room within the married quarters. The police were having some difficulty dealing with him and in an effort to appease him they were willing to accede to his demand that he speak to me. Bloody hell, what good would speaking to me do him I wondered? Anyway, I was duty bound by regulations as orderly officer not to leave camp. So I decided on the obvious solution, I would phone the Field Officer, who was a major, and who lived out of camp and ask him to attend the scene as the situation clearly required a senior ranking officer. As luck would have it the Field Officer did not respond to the phone calls to his home as he was elsewhere, and had not notified the duty personnel of his new location. Things were not looking too good for him either as this was also against regulations. Since the police were adamant that I needed to be at the scene I had no option but to go back to our room and wake up Rusty, very quickly appraise him of the situation, and then deputise him as duty officer while I left camp. I can still hear Rusty's comments as I left the room in some haste - *F****** Scotsmen.* I felt some sympathy with his feelings. Since we were well into the 'wee sma hours' of the night and the married quarters were about one and a half miles distant it was quicker for me to grab my bike and cycle there rather than waken a driver to drive me there. As it so happened it was a freezing cold night with fog in the air and so the saddle of my bike was encrusted with a stiff covering of ice or frozen fog. So there was nothing for it but to cycle there standing up - a bit undignified - but preferable to a wet seat. And so I duly arrived at the married quarters where our erstwhile sergeant major was still haranguing his wife and attempting to gain access to the room wherein she had locked herself. Once I arrived he then transferred his attentions to me and started a long drink-fuelled dialogue with only the occasional intervention from myself. But it was clear that after some time, and after being able to off-load his worries onto me, that he was calming down, such that after what seemed like an eternity, the police were able to gain access to him and put him under arrest without too much altercation. He was then transported to the local police station. It later transpired that his wife asked for all charges against him to be dropped, as she had apparently done on five previous occasions. However, the outcome was that he never appeared back in camp again and I never found out what happened to him. Clearly, the ranks beckoned if he was able to remain in the army, but even that looked to me to be exceedingly doubtful. Naturally, all matters had to be recorded in my report the next morning. As to what action the CO took with the Field Officer who had not notified the duty personnel where he could be contacted I know not, but clearly our CO would have been particularly severe whatever he did. 'SID', as our CO was known behind his back because of the initials in his Christian names, had been promoted from the ranks at Dunkirk, and was not an officer to suffer fools gladly. He was a 'soldier's soldier', both demanding and fair, and he was well respected within the camp. I suspect the field officer suffered more than a severe reprimand.

Immediately prior to this incident our squadron had acquired a new OC, one Major X, who had arrived from a Para Assault Engineer Regiment and was intent on making his presence felt. A new broom, so to speak, who was ever on the lookout to promote himself. Unfortunately, this major did not take kindly to national service men, particularly national service officers. Into the bargain, he was a Roman Catholic, and subalterns of other faiths, or no faiths, were treated in a disdainful manner. If he could put one over on you then he would do so. Things did not look promising for the time remaining until demob.

As was the custom during a sapper's training the party officer took his party out onto the rifle ranges, which were, located not far from Bisley, for a week of intense weapon firing. During this time everyone slept in bivouacs as I have mentioned earlier. For this spell of training .303 rifles and Bren guns were the weapons used. A consequence of this was that we had to have all the weapons and ammunition needed for the weeks training with us in the camp. During periods of High Alert when the IRA was considered to be active, extra security measures were put in place by the party officer to guard against weapons or ammunition being stolen; particularly at night when everyone was 'in the arms of the sandman'. On the ranges where we were training there was a small brick bothy, without doors, which provided a measure of security for the rifles and ammunition. So it was that as I prepared to take out my troop for the weeks weapon training our new OC decided that he must ensure that the security measures that I intended to put in place were sufficient for the task. In principle, there was nothing wrong with that; however, his keen interest aroused my suspicions. He was not just doing his job ensuring that everything would be OK; he clearly had some ulterior motive in mind. So, when we were preparing to go out on the manoeuvres I briefed my sergeant and corporals as to my suspicions about the OC and his interest in our security. Having given the OC my detailed plans for the protection of the weapons and ammunition I then revised the orders to the sergeant and NCOs, and gave them a completely different set of orders with the blunt warning that we had to 'be on our toes' for the duration of the camp. After arriving at the campsite the sappers were also given the revised orders but told nothing about my underlying suspicions. The camp progressed well and the night guards and patrols reported no untoward incidents; that is until the penultimate night. This was when in the early hours of the night our secretive patrols encountered two persons trying to infiltrate the camp, and in particular, the weapons store. A fierce brawl ensued and after a short period of time the two intruders managed to break away from the two-man patrol they had encountered and make their escape. They had been lucky; our patrols were equipped with pick helves and instructed to use them if it was necessary. The intruders were reported to me to have been dressed in camouflage clothing; clearly it looked as if the OC had been up to his tricks wanting to put one over on one of his national service officers. At the end of the week on the ranges I reported back to the OC who, sporting what looked to be suspiciously like a receding black eye, innocently [sic] enquired if there had been any incidents to report. I was more than pleased to be able to detail the incident about the intruders and report that the weapons had been secure at all times. Rather unkindly, I added that I thought that the intrusion had been carried out in a rather amateurish fashion. I later regretted saying this, as I knew, that he knew, that neither of us were being fooled. That evening when I caught up with Rusty I enquired if there had been anything notable that had happened whilst I had been away. *Nothing other than Captain X has gone off sick. He has had a rather nasty accident - a broken arm and ribs and some other bits and pieces…* Now Captain X was a buddy of the OC from 'way back', so it did not take a Sherlock Holmes to realise what had happened. Unsurprisingly, the OC was rather irritable after that and life became that little bit more difficult.

Now the normal procedure on these camps was for the party officer to notify the 'Sally Ann' (Salvation Army) about the manoeuvres, and they would arrange to send a van out on predefined days to allow the sappers to buy their choc bars and any other goodies that they desired to help boost their energy levels during this week living out doors. This was a very good facility, but naturally, the 'Sally Ann' had to charge for the goods and make a very small profit to enable them to continue the service to others. Bearing in mind that these sappers were only earning twenty eight shillings a week (today £1.40p) and that they had to buy Blanco, boot polish, and perhaps even send some money home to a wife or partner, then they had precious little to spend on themselves. So, I arranged with our catering officer, second lieutenant Bill S, that one of my NCOs would collect a prearranged supply of 'goodies' on a sale or return basis, to take to the camp and sell them to the sappers in the evening at NAAFI prices, which were somewhat lower than the 'Sally Ann' prices. This arrangement worked very well and the sappers seemed pleased at this small consideration.

It was about a week or so later that I was summoned to see the OC who was in a particularly nasty mood. The Salvation Army had found out about my arrangements and had been particularly displeased about the affair. Consequently, they had reported the matter to Southern Command, who had contacted our CO, who in turn had contacted my OC for a report on the incident. The OC could smell a chance to pounce on one of his national service officers. A written report was demanded and then he would decide what action had to be taken - most likely, he warned, it would have to go back to the CO for his action. The omens did not look good. So, I prepared a written report outlining the circumstances and the reasons for me doing what I had done - all genuinely in the interests of the troop. When he read the report the OC was not impressed; *against all procedures,* or words to that effect. *Submit the report to the CO,* said he, and at the same time, warning me to be prepared… So it was with more than a little trepidation that I arranged an interview with 'SID' as the CO was known. Now, as I have said previously, he was a hard taskmaster, but fair, and a soldier's soldier. In my presence 'SID' read the report, looked at me sternly, and then enquired if the sappers had been happy with the arrangement. I assured him that they had appreciated it very much. *Good show, but don't do it again. Sir, what about Southern Command?* I managed to mumble - *leave them to me,* and with that I was dismissed. Naturally, the OC was desperate to hear the outcome of my visit to the CO. When I explained what had transpired he couldn't believe it. He was beside himself with an inner rage and could only just keep control of his feelings. He had clearly wanted me reprimanded at the very least. I was happy, but it was another bad omen for the months that lay ahead.

When the sappers reached the end of their 14-week basic training there was the 'Pass off Parade' for those that had completed the course. Naturally, after having been incarcerated for 14 weeks steam had to be let off. Since the course was intensive, time for light entertainment was in short supply. The result of this was that the only time the sappers had free for a pre 'Pass Off' fling was the night before the 'Pass off Parade'. As I have said earlier, this was just about the worst time for such a 'do' - but that was all that the course timings allowed. On these occasions they always wanted a trip to London to celebrate, and maybe even to see a show. So, as was the case, the sappers would decide what they wanted to do, or see, and then the party officer would make the necessary transport and other arrangements since the sappers had no access to the facilities to do this for themselves. As always, we decanted and entrained on the buses somewhere on the Embankment, since it was a central location. The sappers were under strict orders that they had to be back and on at the buses by 11.00 p.m. to allow for the one and a half hour trip back to camp. Reveille the next day was at 6.00 a.m. in preparation for the 'Pass off Parade', so clearly, timings could have been very much better, but such is life. The troop NCOs were always well marshalled to round up stragglers as midnight approached. This was a seemingly impossible task in central London. However, the sappers relied on stories from their predecessors for places to visit/drink, and other activities, so there was a fairly well worn circuit that the NCOs could travel to make sure everyone returned on time. Some of the haunts were well aware that the soldiers were on their first night out in three months and took liberal advantage of them when it came to charging for booze, some of which seemed to me to have been well diluted before being served. The greatest offenders were the

Soho nightclubs where the sappers could partake of some feminine socialising and other activities. One club in particular, whose name I can no longer recall, was a particular favourite. It was on more than one occasion that I had to go into the club and extract the sapper who was partaking rather lustily of the feminine company. Even although we were in civilian clothes the club staff knew full well who you were. *If you would like to have a drink on the house sir we'll extract Sapper Joe Bloggs from the clutches of Susie/Fiona/Flossie* or whoever the hostess was. It was then that you sampled the liquid that was passed off as lager. Sapper Joe Bloggs would then be found looking rather shame faced, but usually non-the worse for wear.

Drinking and fraternising were perfectly acceptable and could be reasonably well monitored; it was when they attended a west end show that it became more difficult. If the show was boring, or a little too high brow for a riotous night out, then voices could be raised with some particularly embarrassing comments about the show. There was one such occasion when I had to order them out of the theatre to let their hair down elsewhere.

It was at the end of one such evening out that everyone assembled at the Embankment prior to midnight and in good time for the journey home. This was in February 1959 and on this particular evening London and the western suburbs were suffering from a real 'pea souper' of a fog; something that was not uncommon at that time. Our bus drivers were always drivers from the Aldershot area and knew the route back to camp like the back of their hand since they had travelled it so often. However, on this night the drivers were extremely agitated about the journey back to camp, and I was no less so. The 'Pass off Parade' could not take place without the sappers. This had all the ingredients of a disaster. There was nothing for it but to set off for camp and do the best we could. Getting out of London was difficult, but slow progress was made. It was when we hit the outer suburbs that we really started to get into trouble and I decided that the best course of action would be for one of the corporals, and myself, to take it in turns to walk ahead of the bus with a torch to help the driver keep to the road, and if possible, the correct side of the road. I remember that at least twice I temporarily lost the bus, even although it had its headlights on. Progress was extremely slow and at one location in particular, where I know not, I could tell that we were on a roundabout, but exactly where on the roundabout I could not tell. It was then that I bumped into another pedestrian, whom up until that point, I had not seen. Thank God, I thought, some one who might be able to give directions. So courteously I asked if he could give any help in pointing us in the direction of Aldershot. *F*** me mate, I live here and I'm f****** lost,* and with that he disappeared into the fog. We were progressing at less than walking pace and time was running out fast. I had no plan 'B'. A Passing Off Parade without the passing off troop did not seem a particularly attractive prospect. However, just as I was beginning to think the unthinkable we broke out of the fog and into a normal dark but clear night. By now we were well into the 'wee sma hours' so it was then that the drivers were told in no uncertain terms *put the bloody foot down.* Fortune was with us and we arrived back in camp about 5.00 a.m. - just in time for reveille at 6.00 a.m. We did get some querulous looks from the guard commander as we entered camp at that rather late hour, and Rusty did wonder what the hell had happened to me as he knew I had reveille at 6.00 a.m. It had been a close run thing. As it so happened, the parade went off very well and everyone was pleased with the display - even the OC. It was only later that evening that I was able to tell Rusty about the events of the previous night. *I thought you bloody Scotsmen would be used to these conditions,* said he displaying a complete lack of sympathy.

As far as I can remember there was only one occasion when we returned to camp minus a sapper. On that occasion an exhaustive search of the usual haunts had proved to be fruitless and so we had no option but to set off for camp one hour or so later than planned, and minus one sapper. Things were not looking too good for that recruit. As events turned out he made it back to camp under his own steam and just in time for reveille. I informed him that he could join the party for the 'Passing off Parade' and that I would deal with his misdemeanour after the ceremonial duties were over. It turned out that he had missed our buses at the Embankment for reasons outwith his control. To his credit he had used his 'sapper initiative' and pulled out all the stops to get himself back to camp just in time for reveille, and for that he deserved great credit. Once the parade was over he was due to go on leave and then onwards to his next posting. The end result was that I told him that under any other circumstances he would have been 'on a fizzer' but the administrative hassle of carrying the charge over to his next regiment was not worth the hassle. He got a good earful and was sent on his way. Secretly, I was well pleased with the initiative and drive he had shown getting himself back to camp in the prevailing circumstances. He would undoubtedly mature into a good sapper.

School of Military Engineering, Gordon Barracks, Gillingham, Kent

In November 1958, just as things were starting to get a bit more fraught with the OC who was constantly niggling at some of us national service subalterns, I received a summons from him to report to his office. He then told me that he had been instructed that I was to attend an interview with the CO the next day. What had I been up to he enquired? I was bemused - why would the CO want to see me. I did not know. Clearly, the OC did not believe me. *Report back to me once you have seen the CO* was his instruction. That night when I met up with Rusty in the mess I told him the tale only to find that he had been likewise summonsed to see the CO. In Rusty's case his OC was not in the least bothered what his young officer had been up to.

So the next day it was with great trepidation that we presented ourselves at the adjutant's office a little before the appointed hour in the hope that he might be able to give us an early warning as to why the CO might want to see us; but the adjutant was just as much in the dark as were. When summonsed, in we went, and were more than a little surprised that we were invited to have a seat. This certainly took us by surprise. *What do you have planned for the next four weeks* he enquired? Well what indeed we wondered; and so we mumbled out the usual stories about being up to our eyes in training, and admin, and all the usual claptrap, but he was clearly not listening. *Well, I want you two to represent me and the 2IC of the regiment on a field-engineering course at Brompton Barracks in Chatham*, which was the Headquarters of the Corps of Royal Engineers. *Can you do that?* This seemed like a bloody silly question - did we have a choice? Naturally, we both showed enthusiasm for the ploy. Four weeks away from camp seemed a great idea. *Here are the details of the course.* And with that he handed over the documentation for us to quickly browse before being dismissed. Nano seconds later we were both nonplussed. *Sir, this course is for senior officers of Lt Colonel and above. Never mind that, I'll sort everything out. The 2IC and I are too busy to attend.* We managed to stammer out a few more splutterings about being thoroughly out ranked, but he was having none of it. *And by the way, give my regards to Brigadier ? when you meet him and tell him I'm disappointed that I cannot attend the course.* And with that we were out the door. *Hells bells Rusty, I'm bloody apprehensive about this.* Rusty was no less apprehensive.

As I had been instructed I reported back to my OC regarding what had transpired and gave him all the details. *Nonsense, nonsense, you can't go on this course, it's for very senior officers.* Well I knew that, but he was not deterred. *Leave this to me* he muttered, seething with rage, *I'll see the CO.* It was very clear that he wanted to take my place and attend the course himself. It was the perfect vehicle for self-promotion, and a bit of sucking up to some more senior officers. A few days later I enquired the outcome of his meeting with the CO as I had preparations to make if I was still going on the course. *Its all right, I've cleared it with the CO for you to attend.* Some tale; he had obviously been given a flea in his ear and told to b****r off. Naturally, he was not at all pleased with me even although I had had no active part in any of the proceedings.

So, on the appointed day, Rusty and I made our way to Brompton Barracks and signed in at reception, although the training course was to be shared between Brompton Barracks and Gordon Barracks. A few eyebrows were raised when it was clear we could only muster four pips between us, but nothing was said. When it came time to assemble for the introduction to the course, which was on Advanced Field Engineering, it was clear that we were the odd ones out. There were no other pips in sight, only crowns and crossed swords, red-banded service caps and gold braid, but of another pip there were none. The officers assembled were from all corners of the Commonwealth. From India, Pakistan I think, Canada, Australia, many Brits and a few others. Generals of all denominations were there, some of whom looked as if they had been desk bound for quite some time.

The next day we started on the course which covered all aspects of field engineering, from Bailey bridging to mine clearance, and everything else as well. Naturally, the more senior officers tended to 'pull rank' when it came to the more physical aspects of the course. This was particularly so with the ones from India and Pakistan who delighted in getting us two *young whipper snappers* to do the needful on their behalf; but it was all done with a great degree of humour. And so the course progressed with a lot of cursing from the senior ranks, and with Rusty and I having to work our socks off complying with all their instructions when they 'copped out' of many of the physical tasks, but we didn't mind; it was no great sweat to us having done much of it before in the recent past. The plus side came in the evenings when we all dined together in the mess. The Colonials were particularly generous when it came to dishing out free rounds of booze knowing that as national service types our pay was 'sweet Fanny Adams'. No rank was pulled in the mess, but we knew full well to show due deference lest we could be on a hiding to nothing.

However, the most embarrassing part of the course came when we were assembled to be instructed on the latest and most secret items of the army's explosive devices. Then it was decreed that only those with a security clearance of a sufficiently high rating would be allowed to attend the lecture and demonstrations. Rusty and I were admitted without any problems having been security vetted fairly recently, but when it came to some of the Canadian and Australian senior officers they were debarred because they did not have the necessary clearance. How this could be we did not know, but naturally these officers were raging that we two 'subbies' should have admittance and they were barred. Afterwards, Rusty and I did not feel that the lecture justified the restriction on these officers, but it was not in our power to do other than accept the situation. There was a deal more tension in the mess for a few nights after that incident. Rusty and I were careful to mind our 'Ps and Qs' for a bit.

During one of the mess nights we were able to meet Brigadier ? whom our CO had mentioned and we passed on his best wishes together with a little bit of flattery on the side. It was clear that they had been very good buddies and had been through much together. At least we could now report back to 'SID' that we had done as he wished.

Sometime during the course I also met a major who was the OC of a territorial engineer squadron in Edinburgh, and knowing that I was from the city he offered me the chance to join his squadron. I was really quite pleased to have been asked and up to that point I had never contemplated joining the Territorial Army on my release from national service. However, the thought was short lived. After a very little contemplation I diplomatically declined his offer.

At the start of the course it had struck me that my OC would want to know all that had happened, and whom we had met, so both Rusty and I agreed that it would be wise to keep a diary during the course, and as it progressed, write up the report. This was me trying to keep one step ahead of the OC and be prepared when he asked me, as I knew he would, for a report on my four weeks 'swanning around'. And so it was that at the end of the course which we had greatly enjoyed, we had to return to camp, quite sad that it had all come to an end. For starters, no more free drinks in the mess.

As I had anticipated the OC was ever curious and had to be told of all the top brass that we had met and did anyone enquire about him? Fat chance… Naturally, he had to have a written report as well. But I was ahead of him. On my return I had asked the Squadron Clerk to have my report typed out in duplicate, and so I was ready for his request, which took him by surprise. Nothing daunted, he felt that it must be presented to the CO. So, feeling that I could not go it alone, Rusty and I arranged to meet the CO and appraise him of the course and submit our reports to him. He seemed pleased and said that he would read them with interest; but he was most pleased when we reported that we had met his old buddy, Brigadier ?, and had passed on his good wishes. As we left his office I could see out of the corner of my eye our reports winging their way to his waste paper bin.

All in all, it had been a very enjoyable four weeks.

3TRRE, Guillemont Barracks, Cove, Hampshire

It was the first week in December when we got back from the course only to find that a mess dance had been arranged for Friday 5 December and that all the subalterns had to organise the dance and decorate the mess. Unfortunately, I was orderly officer the day before the dance and did not get to my bed until 2.00 a.m., and then at 3.30 a.m. I had to attend at the guardroom for some minor incident, so sleep was in short supply on the day of the dance. After attending to all the normal duties we 'subbies' then had to attend the dance which started at 7.30 p.m., and it did not finish until 4.00 a.m. Now for some reason I had volunteered some weeks earlier to do orderly officer on the day after the dance, not being aware at that time that a dance was on the cards, so for three days I barely saw my bed.

My party had just 'Passed Off' some days earlier making it a hectic few weeks, so it was with some relief that I had a week or more to catch up on admin. prior to taking a sergeant and a few corporals to Malvern to collect my next intake.

It was a very cold and befuddled set of recruits that were assembled on the platform of Malvern Station at 6.30 a.m. that very cold and dreich Monday morning. The low mist and cloud that I remembered as a recruit many months before still appeared to be lingering around. Then, sometime later in the day I was given the sheet with the recruits names and on it I recognised a name that was uncommon, but familiar to me. Surely it couldn't be Dave X, someone who had been at school with me and had been more than a swot. A bit of a 'brain box' who firmly eschewed helping anyone when they did not fully understand the physics questions. For this reason he wasn't always terribly popular. Sure enough it was he. After completing his degree with first class honours in engineering, he had been recruited by 'Betty Windsor' for his stint in khaki. He had never been a terribly physical person at school and here in the cold light of day he looked decidedly out of place. He was even more perplexed when he realised that for the duration, I was now his Party Officer. It was clear from the outset that whatever lay ahead the sappers were not for Dave. And so it transpired that after passing basic training - just - he later managed to transfer to the Education Corp; something to which he was much more suited. It was five decades later, when I discovered that he lived in the same city as myself, that I made an effort to contact him by email. It was with some regret that I found out afterwards why he had not returned my approach. He had died just a few weeks before I had emailed him. Such is life!

1959

Life's not so bad after all

After a very brief New year leave I was back at camp, but this time asking the CO for permission to get married. It was a requirement of all officers - at least at that time - that the CO's permission had to be obtained before getting married. Clearly, there was no reason for him to withhold this permission, and so it was granted. Consequently, this meant that there were various arrangements to be made, such as getting the banns called in the local church in Cove and arranging to purchase a 'going away' suit, etc., etc. However, it must be said that 90%, if not more, of the arrangements were made by Lorna back home. I had the easy bit; I just had to turn up on the appointed day and say, *I do.*

Royal Army Medical Corps, Keogh Barracks, Ash Vale, Hampshire

After the 'Passing off Parade' of a party there was usually a two-week period before the troop officer took charge of another new intake, and during this time you had the opportunity to catch up on admin. tasks that had had to take a back seat during the long training period. There was also the chance that you might be sent on a short course during this 'down time'. Such was the case when one squad passed off that the OC informed me that a place had arisen for a short course on first aid and that he had detailed me to attend. The course was based at Keogh Barracks, home of the Royal Army Medical Corp, and was taking place the following day. Well, first aid was not my thing but at least I could savour the delights of another regiment for eight days, which was the duration of the course.

The course itself turned out to be quite interesting, but naturally, it was all based around injuries sustained in battle. The course was attended by all ranks and from various regiments. One attendee got very short shrift when he asked if we would be instructed in how to deliver a baby. The displays that the instructors laid on to simulate battle injuries were nothing less than gob smacking. The skill in replicating broken bones, bloody wounds and other injuries were outstanding. Attending to these casualties when in a smoke filled dugout with thunder flashes going off around you made the realism even more dramatic. The first time they introduced us to these scenes a burly sergeant major from one of the guards regiments passed out. But no opportunity was lost - here was a chance for the medics to show us how to treat someone who had fainted. Otherwise, the course passed off fairly uneventfully and the break away from camp had been refreshing. I just hoped that when I returned to camp I was not going to be asked to demonstrate all the various skills that had been acquired. Fortunately, I was not asked.

3TRRE, Guillemont Barracks, Cove, Hampshire

It was at the end of this first aid course, early on a Wednesday morning, when I had just returned to camp, that I had a message waiting for me to see the OC. These messages never had a good feel to them.

So, dutifully, I got myself organised and then reported to the OC in the squadron office. There were a few perfunctory enquiries about the first aid course and then he got down to the 'nitty gritty'. *Chic, morale in the squadron is low.* Well tell me something new I thought. Since he had arrived an excellent squadron had taken a bit of a nosedive, morale wise. *I have arranged a squadron dance in the NAFFI for Saturday evening.* My thoughts immediately flashed along the lines of - *oh, bloody hell man, we have three hundred sex starved sappers in the squadron and no females whatsoever.* At which point I was way ahead of him. My thoughts were racing ahead at double speed; surely he's not going to ask me to…, but he was. *Chic, we need three hundred females for the dance on Saturday night and it's up to you to get them.* The think bubbles coming out of my head were unprintable, and certainly not complimentary as far as he was concerned. *Any ideas sir I enquired hopefully? That's up to you Chic.* There was nothing for it but to get on with it; but where to start? After some brief cogitations I decided that the best thing to do would be to see the transport officer, second lieutenant Bill S, and get the use of a 'champ' - the army equivalent of the jeep in those days - and a driver who was familiar with the Aldershot area. Bill very kindly acceded to my request with the rather barbed comment - *good luck mate, better you than me.* Fortunately, he was able to provide a driver who knew the area well and so together we sat down with the telephone book (no yellow pages in those days) and some other reference documents and ploughed through them to establish all the work places that had an abundance of female employees. Huntley & Palmer in Reading, as I recall, was one employer that I decided to target - but there were many others as well. Naturally, it was those employing the largest numbers of employees that I targeted first.

So, I gave the driver free reign to map out the best and most efficient route to allow us to visit all of the places that we thought might be a fruitful source of talent. It was clearly going to take more than a day to visit them all; but an even bigger headache loomed ahead. How was I going to get the girls from various pick up points around the county and get them to 3TRRE; and then even more problematical, get them home again? However, that was a headache for tomorrow. Time was now of the essence and I still had to get three hundred girls; so we set off to visit all the various places on our list.

At each location I sought a meeting with the personnel officer or the equivalent. As it so transpired, things went very well and everyone I approached seemed rather amused at the thought, and were more than willing to try to round up a few heads on my behalf. I seem to recollect that the aforementioned Huntley & Palmer were the most fruitful source and were able to tell me that they thought they could get a sizeable proportion of the numbers that I wanted. This was extremely encouraging news. Visits to the other establishments were less fruitful, but I was still able to garner a few heads here and there. By the midday on Thursday I was well on my way to getting the three hundred, but I was still a little short on numbers and I had only one place on my list left to visit. It was the training depot or barracks of the QUARANCS (Queen Alexandra's Army Nursing Corps). I cannot remember where they were based but it sticks in my mind that it was somewhere beginning with H; Hindhead, or some similar sounding name. When we arrived there it didn't seem the most inviting of establishments, but I couldn't be choosy; so I asked to see the Adjutant. After a somewhat formal interrogation she decided that I would have to see the Commanding Officer. So it was that I was ushered into the presence of this rather forbidding figure; I think she was a 'half colonel'.

I then had to go through my spiel again to a rather bemused Lieutenant Colonel. Why were we having a dance, why this, why that? But at last she relented and said that she might be able to release about twenty or so of her more senior recruits. This was excellent news. *Just one stipulation lieutenant. Yes Ma'am. I want your guarantee that you will return them 'virgo intacta'.* As best as I could I explained that this was one stipulation that no one could guarantee; but I assured her that I would make my very best endeavours. She reluctantly accepted my explanation and I got my twenty or so recruits; but how I was going to guarantee their virginity I had no idea.

Now came the even more difficult task of organising the collection and transportation of the girls on the day, and then the return journey back home in the evening. Fortunately, after explaining the situation to the OC he was able to pull some rank with his counterpart in Headquarters Squadron and I was allocated a number of TCVs for the task. In addition, he allowed a small sum of money to be spent on a couple of hire buses to augment the TCVS. On the night of the dance I think we managed to assemble about 290 of the 300 girls that had been targeted. I was pretty dammed pleased. To my surprise the dance went off rather well and everyone, including the OC, was more than happy.

I still of course had to get the girls back from whence they had come. For this task I had assembled all my NCOs and some more besides. When I explained to them the request from the QUARANCS commanding officer there was hearty laughter all round. *We're on a sticky wicket there Sir.* I had to agree with their comments, and innuendo. *We are, but we'll damned well try.* So when the dance finished the NCOs were in there with vigour assembling the masses and disentangling the more amorous of the sappers, which in some cases meant digging them out of the bushes and undergrowth that was around the perimeter of the camp. Surprisingly, it all went rather well and all bodies were returned to their various destinations. Whether *virgo intacta* or not, I did not know, but it made good sense not to enquire.

Actions of course, have their reactions. About a week or so after the dance I got a summons to see the OC with another of those 'something is wrong' feelings. He was not best pleased when I saw him. *You have been reported to Southern Command for driving on roads which are out of bounds. The CO wants a report.* I suspected the CO merely wanted an explanation and not a written report, but I was in no position to argue. The background to the situation was that in Southern Command, orders were issued each week and embedded within these orders would be restrictions on driving on certain roads within the region. Usually this was because they were small country roads, or roads populated with houses of a certain standing. To anyone not familiar with the area it was an absolute nightmare trying to keep track of all these minor roads that were forbidden to military traffic, so it meant relying on the driver to be fully up-to-date with the restrictions, and most, if not all, were extremely good at this. So, when I had been out a week earlier trying to amass three hundred young ladies for the dance I had, under pressure of time, instructed my driver to take a road that was restricted since I felt that there was no option if I was going to recruit all the young ladies needed. Initially, he had been apprehensive because it was the driver's responsibility to obey the Southern Command restrictions, but I told him that he was acting under my orders and that I would take the consequences. In truth, I thought that no one would notice - but I was wrong. Someone had spotted us and reported the incident to Southern Command who had traced the offending vehicle back to our camp. The complaint having come from Southern Command meant the CO had no recourse but to find out what had happened. I explained to my OC the circumstances but he was adamant that a full written report must be submitted to the CO as it was out of his hands. Clearly, he wanted to make the most of the situation and was relishing the prospect of hanging one of his young national service officers out to dry. Naturally, I completed the report as fast as I could and put the best spin on it that I possibly could. I was then ordered to make an appointment with the CO and deliver the report to him in person, and this I did. It was always a formidable occasion to be summoned to meet 'SID' and this time was certainly no exception. After giving him the report he read it, and then re-read it. Paused for a moment, and then asked for the details of the situation in my own words. I duly explained the circumstances again and repeated that the driver had warned me about the prohibition order but that I had instructed him to drive on. 'SID', who was of the 'men and horses first' school of officers, thought for a moment then enquired about the dance and asked if it gone well? I told him it had been a success. At that I was instructed not to do it again, and dismissed. Before departing I enquired about Southern Command. *Leave them to me.* As I departed the room I'm sure I saw my report fluttering gently towards the waste paper basket. Boy, was I relieved?

Naturally, the OC was desperate to know the outcome of my interview with the CO, so I gave him a very full rundown of the interview. He was aghast. *Has the CO not reprimanded you?"* "*No Sir.*

He was furious and at a loss for words, but with the CO having dealt with the situation there was nothing he could do. It was a narrow escape to be sure.

It was sometime later that I discovered that the offending road had been close to Islington Mill near Alton in Hampshire, the residence of the retired Field Marshall Montgomery. He was always known as a crotchety old b****r, the more so in his retirement. No prizes for guessing who had reported me.

Soon afterwards, in late March 1959, I was off on a two-week spell of leave as I was getting married. Naturally, there was the obligatory stag party, which was held at the Frensham Ponds Hotel. As might be imagined it was a good night. Everyone drove there and back - goodness knows what the drink driving laws were at that time but I suspect there were none, or precious few. Rusty dutifully saw me back to camp at the end of the evening and arranged a battery of fire buckets around my bed for the inevitable aftermath, having been aware that I had had twenty-three brandy sours! No guesses what I felt like the next day. As for 'Taff' our Welsh batman, he was horrified to see the mess, which I assured him I would attend to when I was compos mentis once more. He was disgusted that his young charges could behave in this fashion. Fortunately, this all took place a week before I was heading north for the wedding. The wedding date as it transpired, had unfortunately landed in the middle of the training period of my party, which meant that I had to be away during a critical stage of their training. However, the OC had managed to get a stand-in for me; someone who would then carry on to be a 2IC to me for a period of time.

The replacement was a newly commissioned officer from Sandhurst. This seemed to me to be a very satisfactory arrangement, that is, until he arrived. He drove up in a large, open-topped, vintage Lagonda sports car, with headlamps the size of which would have put small searchlights to shame; and sporting a double-barrelled name to boot. Worse still, his attitude was particularly snooty. He apparently thought he was God's gift to the army. After appraising him of the duties ahead, and having a quiet word with my sergeant, I departed on leave with a good deal of foreboding. As expected, the wedding and honeymoon went well. One of the few entries in my diary for that time lists the fact that the one week stay in the Royal Oak Hotel in Keswick (sadly no longer) for the both of us cost a princely £36-14-0p of which 3/- was for minerals, and that my new suit from Burtons had depleted our savings by £14-10-0p. So how did we manage this vast expenditure - I have absolutely no idea? The good news was that as a married officer my pay increased to, I think, £11 per week or thereby - 'riches beyond avarice'! But the good times had to end and after the honeymoon I had to head back to camp, more than a little reluctantly, and with even more stomach churning goodbyes in Waverley Station.

When I made contact again with the troop on the Monday of my return the sense of gloom was palpable. The young stand-in deputy had done nothing of any note. Two sappers in particular who had had financial problems back home had gone to see him for help and advice had been dismissed out of hand and told to sort it out themselves. Clearly, this was impractical, as these soldiers did not have the time or facilities to do so. It did not take much to bring the morale of a troop down when the men were being worked harder than they had ever done in their lives and their well-being was being ignored. The NCOs were all equally despondent as he had ignored their experience in certain situations and had gone his own sweet way. Fortunately, the OC was curious to know how the wedding had gone, and more particularly, how the young stand in was doing. I suspected that he knew full well how he was faring but was awaiting confirmation from me. Without trying to denigrate our young blood too much I sought the most diplomatic language I could muster to emphasise that his rare talents would be better deployed elsewhere, preferably in another regiment. Clearly, the OC was of a similar mind and after a quiet word with the CO the matter was quickly resolved and our young friend was posted to pastures new. It took a bit of midnight oil to un-entangle the various personal problems that had arisen, but it was accomplished. The sappers only needed to see that something was being done on their behalf for morale to start to pick up again.

Sometime around this period the police reported that there had been some serious crime in the village of Cove, which was adjacent to our camp. So one evening the whole camp was paraded on the parade ground with every man accounted for and an identity parade took place. Fortunately, no one in our camp or the adjacent camp of Southwood was identified as the miscreant, because it was normally the case that by default, army personnel would be blamed until the real culprit had been found.

One unfortunate incident around this time concerned Sapper X. Sapper X was a good soldier, but a bit introverted. He had made it through the first four weeks of training, had reported no problems, and appeared to be progressing reasonably well. One night one of the sappers who shared the same room as Sapper X got up in the middle of the night to use the toilet facilities. When he entered the ablutions area he found Sapper X there having already rigged up some cord from one of the rafters and preparing to make a suicide attempt on his life. The sapper immediately raised the alarm and Sapper X was restrained from succeeding with his attempt. After due process Sapper X was transferred to Cambridge Military Hospital for treatment. We later heard that he had responded well to his time there and was able to be discharged from hospital some weeks later. The cause of the problem, it transpired, was because Sapper X had personal problems at home and he had not been willing to share these problems with anyone, not even those back home. When the cause was determined, and, as far as I am aware, resolved, then Sapper X made a speedy recovery and was able to resume military duties. This incident merely highlighted the fact that no matter how hard you tried to ensure that the sappers' personal problems were being dealt with, ultimately, they had to make you aware of their troubles so that remedial action could be attempted.

In cases such as this where the problem lay outwith my area of influence I could at least engage the services of SSAFA to see what help they could provide. SSAFA was a voluntary organisation - Soldiers, Sailors, & Airmen Families Association - run, as far as I remember, by wives of senior service personnel. Because they had representatives in most of the more populated parts of the UK they could offer local help and advice to the families of service personnel who had domestic problems.

Junior Officer Efficiency Tests

Towards the end of 1958 the desk bound brass in Southern Command decided that they should run Junior Officer Efficiency Tests (JOETs) in the late spring of 1959, with each regiment in the Aldershot Garrison Area competing against one another. Our regiment, 3TRRE, was pretty laid back about the whole affair but some regiments selected teams and put them into full time training for the event. At 3TRRE we fitted in training between duties and were not too despondent if we missed a session or two. However, as time went on and the news started to filter back to the CO that other regiments had officers in full time training he started to encourage a more active regime, which meant everything from route marches, to wireless drill, motorcycle training and emergency vehicle repairs, swimming and everything else under the sun.

As the test period drew closer a small team of four was picked to be the representatives of 3TRRE with, as I recollect a couple of standbys. Try as I might I couldn't get out of the team - everyone else had managed to devise a better excuse than I could muster, so I was in the team. The physical side of the test was not a problem as I was extremely fit due to the fact that I regularly took part in the troop route marches and the assault course training, but the motorcycle riding I did not like. I seemed to be on the ground more that I was on the bike and the army motorcycles were dammed heavy to restore to an upright position once fallen. But the training, such as it was, continued in our own time. Into the bargain, I did my own running in full Battle Order in the woods behind the Officers' Mess, so I was fit enough to cope with what might be thrown at us.

So, on a warm day in late May 1959 fourteen or more four-man teams assembled at 8.00 a.m. at predetermined rendezvous to take part in the JOETs. The national service officers in our team were not greatly motivated when we heard that the winning team was to have tea with the General Officer Commanding the Aldershot Garrison Area. Hmmm! A dubious honour we thought and one that we would be happy to miss out on.

So, at the appointed hour, we were all kitted out in full Battle Order and armed with our less than trusty Sten guns. A particular nuisance was the tin helmet that had to be worn or carried. Anyone familiar with 'doubling' on a route march wearing a tin hat and carrying full kit will be well acquainted with the discomfort this bit of ill-fitting kit can cause.

The first part of the test was a route march, or jog, of 11 miles followed by another three miles across country. The first 11 miles were covered by 'Shank's Pony' at the fastest speed of the slowest member of the team. The next three miles of cross-country navigation did indeed involve a pony, or a horse, to be more precise. Awaiting us at the start of this three-mile section was the said horse, a motorcycle, a bicycle and a Champ army vehicle, which had been partially disabled by the removal of the distributor cap. It then fell to each of us in the team to choose our method of travel over the three-mile stretch using our choice of transport. Fortunately, in our team we had a subaltern who was a keen horseman, so he got to ride the horse. We also had two 'petrol heads' in the team, so they quickly choose their preferred vehicle. Thus, I was left with the bicycle, which suited me fine. I had never been on a horse before and our preparations, such as they had been, had not considered this possibility. I was also extremely glad that Frank W was keen to ride the motorcycle and Bill B was eager to use the 'Champ'. The missing distributor cap did not fool Bill one bit as he immediately spotted the malfunction and put it to rights. These three miles proved to be extremely tough going and the bike, as I soon discovered, was not at all suited to the terrain. Consequently, I was carrying it and all the kit more than I was riding it. When we reached the target spot we were then helicoptered for five miles to another area where we had to navigate our way through some dense woodland to another rendezvous point. Our map reading over this stretch of the course was tested to its limits as there were no obvious features on the ground that allowed us to check our bearings. However, we made it in good time and without any frayed tempers - always a good thing in a small team. At the end of this stretch we then had some target shooting with our Sten guns, and with our pistols, which we were also carrying. The accuracy of a Sten gun as I have previously said, leaves much to be desired, but when you are tired it can all become a bit more problematical. Nevertheless, our shooting was pretty respectable. After this we then had to travel another mile across country to a spot where there were some simulated battle casualties. Having been on the first aid course sometime before, this proved to be a gift from heaven as far as I was concerned, and as a team we were able to deal with the various injuries at some speed, and with a little skill. My attendance at the first aid course had been extremely fortuitous and stood us in good stead.

Then we were off again navigating over another three and a half miles across country to our next rendezvous. At this point we found a broken down military truck that had been deliberately disabled. Our task was to get the truck running again. Our two 'petrol heads' were well up to the task - thank God for Bill and Frank. After this we then had to climb a hill, where it was I cannot remember, and then we had to send some wireless signals in code from the sets provided at the rendezvous point. Having completed this task we were then given a lift in a TCV to Hawley

Lake, our old stamping ground, to do some watermanship. Here we were given an assortment of planks, rope, oil drums, and a few bits and bobs. Our task was to build a raft and transport the four of us, plus kit, plus a heavy anchor, 150 yards across the lake to the island and to keep all our kit and the anchor dry. My diary records that we did this in 20 minutes and with perfectly dry kit; but individually we were all 'somping wet'. We then had to get back across the lake to terra firma once more and then hoof it to the assault course. With full kit and dripping wet BDs, and tired as well, the assault course proved to be harder than it normally was, but still we completed it in a satisfactory time. Nearby to the assault course we were given four ground sheets and some rope or cord, together with a collection of potatoes, eggs, carrots, cabbage and some tinder. A couple of bivis had to be built and a fire started and the food cooked into some edible form. Since we had only had some chocolate bars between us all day the small amount of cooked food went down a treat. We were later informed that we had not been meant to eat the cooked meal - ah well, it had tasted good even if points would be deducted from our score. So, the day ended well and we were then helicoptered back to our original start point, which was a long way from our camp. So, having been adjacent to our 3TRRE, we now had to make the long journey back to our base, still very wet. Whatever else a battle dress had been designed for, waterproofing was not one of its strong points. On the other hand its designer would have been well pleased with its water retention properties. We did not win tea with the general, oh dear me!, but I think our team were placed either third or fourth in the competition, so we were well satisfied. No more JOETs until next May, and by then we would be well and truly back in 'civvy street'.

3TRRE, Guillemont Barracks, Cove, Hampshire

Summer 1959 was a particularly hot summer and it was on one 'Block Weekend' in June that Rusty and I volunteered to do

Orderly Officer duty over the long weekend leave allowing me to take my leave at a time that fitted in with the local statutory holidays in Edinburgh. On this weekend Rusty and I were looking forward to a lazy break with an almost deserted camp and a much-relaxed atmosphere. Things were looking promising with the hot weather, that is, until the Saturday afternoon when it was my turn to be 'orderly dog'. It was then that I got a message to report to the guardroom. At the guard room the guard commander was in conversation with an agitated sapper who had been sent in from the training ranges with a request for help. The small group that were out in the training area had encountered fires breaking out and had requested help to put the fires out before they became dangerous. So, without hesitation I immediately sent off a runner to round up the various sappers that were on standby duty as firemen for the weekend. The duty squad were soon assembled and dispatched out to the training area in the camp fire engine. This was a vehicle that had been declared a relic 'many moons' before, but which could still do a job when needed. Satisfied, I returned for a bit of relaxation prior to the next round of inspections. Not too long had passed before there was another summons to the guardroom. Again the same sapper, but looking decidedly more agitated. *I've been told to tell you Sir that it is getting bloody dangerous. Can you come out and see what's happening?* Fortunately, Rusty was in camp and I was able to task him as orderly officer whilst I was out of camp. He was not best pleased that his sunbathing had been interrupted. So it was onto my trusty bike and out to the training ground. This was a bike that I had bought second hand from a subaltern who was getting demobbed and which I was later able to sell to my successor for the same price a year and a half later.

Once out on the ranges I soon saw the problem. The gorse fire was rapidly getting out of control and was moving erratically here there and everywhere, but the worst bit was the exploding ammunition. These training areas had been in use from WWII when live rounds were used in training and when little effort had been made at the time to retrieve spent or unused rounds. As I wrote earlier, efforts had been made at a much later date to clear the ground of this danger, particularly in the firing ranges, but trying to find every live round in the other areas had been like looking for needles in haystacks. Well, we were now finding these live rounds and boy were they 'giving it laldy'. There was no pattern to the small explosions that were taking place everywhere. The corporal in charge had been right - it was bloody dangerous. There was nothing for it but to withdraw the troops and let the fire burn out. Fortunately, there were natural fire barriers in place that would prohibit the spread of the fire to other areas. That weekend most of the army ranges and training areas within the Aldershot Garrison area were affected to a greater or lesser degree by these wild fires. Our small group had been helpless to make more than a token gesture in the fight against the flames.

It was sometime in the early summer of 1959 when Rusty was on orderly officer duty that one night, in the early hours, he discovered a small troop of marine commandos in camouflage clothing preparing to make an attempt to infiltrate our explosives store in the woods. It was an exercise to test the state of alertness of our security systems in case of an IRA raid. When he became aware of intruders Rusty got the driver of his 'champ' vehicle to park some distance away from the group and he made his approach secretly on foot. Prior to doing so he had commandeered the driver's Lee Enfield rifle and made sure that there was a round 'up the spout'. Stealthily, he was able to take them by surprise even although they were hiding in the undergrowth. When challenged to come out they at first laid low in an effort to fool him into thinking that no one was there. Nothing daunted, Rusty told them he would open fire if they did not come out with their hands on their heads, and to emphasise that he meant business, he fired a round high into the nearest tree. As it transpired, the sergeant in charge of the squad was operating as a lookout in the lower reaches of the tree. Rusty was never sure who got the greatest fright - the sergeant or himself as he dropped from the tree in a state of shock. The remaining members of the squad immediately emerged from the undergrowth extremely apprehensive that they may also be shot at. Rusty, in rather gentlemanly fashion, gave the sergeant a lift in the back of the 'champ' back to our barracks whilst the remainder of the squad had to run behind the vehicle. Rusty was then able to contact their base and arrange for transport to come and collect them. It was a rather crestfallen squad of commandos that left 3TRRE that night. Rusty still can't remember how he legitimised the firing of a live round without first having followed the procedure on his little yellow card.

Later in 1959, Rusty got the slightly more unusual task of having to organise a concert for the camp and one of the groups he managed to get to perform were the *Mudlarks*. The *Mudlarks* had been a well-known pop group in 1958, and indeed, they had had two Top Ten Singles during this period. However, in late 1958 Jeff Mudd was enlisted for national service and, as it so happened, he was posted to our camp. By the time he had finished training in 1959 he was then taken onto the permanent staff of the camp, since it was foreseen that any talented person was a benefit to the camp. The *Mudlarks* meanwhile had continued to perform, having enlisted another singer to take Jeff's place for the duration of his national service. So, as well as being able to assemble a talented group of permanent staff from the camp to perform at the concert, to have a Top Ten Pop Group perform as well was the 'icing on the cake'. Rusty was thoroughly chuffed; even more so when he was summoned by some Brigadier in Aldershot, who, having heard who was performing, asked Rusty if he would chaperone his daughter to the concert with the bonus that he would be allowed the use of the Brigadier's car to get them both to and from the concert. We in the mess were all slightly envious. Was she going to be a real stunner we wondered? Naturally, Rusty made every effort to look his best on the day and before going to collect her took the precaution of taking a small bouquet of flowers for his companion to be. What a chancer we all thought. He was more than a little deflated when it turned out that the daughter was only nine years old. The cries of 'baby snatcher' rang in his ears for a few days thereafter. But the upside was that the concert had been a huge success and the young girl had proved to be entertaining company. The Brigadier and his daughter were delighted, Rusty's OC was pleased, and Rusty himself was much relieved that everything had gone as planned. I seem to recollect that Rusty stood us a few beers in the mess after the concert was over.

As I have already commented, in the down time between intakes it was the norm to catch up on any administrative backlog and to attend courses that had to be taken. For the NCOs it was also a time that they could be sent on a course, should one be available. Otherwise, time could hang a bit more heavily for them if they did not have any leave to take. So, whenever possible, I tried to arrange for tasks for them to carry out whenever they had some free time. My letters home at that time show that during one of these breaks between intakes I set an initiative test for my NCOs which I designed to last for three days. They were charged with travelling across the south of England, at their own expense, to carry out certain tasks at pre determined spots. Tasks that I was able to verify that they had carried out correctly. Food and sleeping arrangements they had to make on the hoof, again at their own expense. I assumed that they would have sought out the nearest army barracks to wherever they had to go and plead for food and a bunk for the night - but that was up to them. They had to use their 'sapper initiative'. They could sleep under the stars if that was their choice. Each corporal was given a separate set of tasks to carry out and so they each had different destinations to travel to; consequently, they were on their own. What the various tasks were I cannot remember, but the outing seemed to be relished by all with each achieving the allotted objectives. It did not surprise me as I had an extremely competent set of NCOs, the more senior of whom would surely make it to sergeant at some later date. Naturally, Sergeant H, my Party Sergeant, being of greater seniority than the other NCOs was excused this frivolity.

Nevertheless, no matter how competent a bunch of NCOs you had, it was always necessary to be on alert in case of any flagging of standards. One such case arose when one of the sappers had transgressed and had been given a 'drying room' punishment. At the time I was slightly suspicious of the fact that perhaps the transgression had not quite merited this punishment. So, on that particular evening I returned to the spider to check on what was happening to discover that the sapper, having got slightly 'bolshy', was in the process of getting a double session of punishment. At that point I had to quietly draw one of the NCOs aside and tell him that there would be no double sessions - one was quite sufficient. Even the most hardy of souls would be felled by a double session in the drying room. Naturally, this cessation of punishment was done without the sapper realising that I had intervened. It was always bad man management to counteract an NCOs orders in front of sappers, as he still had to maintain discipline and have their respect - if that is the appropriate word.

Being with a training regiment meant that 'bull' and turnout was always uppermost in everyone's thoughts and minds and sappers had to be on the alert lest some marauding NCO collared them for some small and niggling offence. As I said earlier, Nos. 6 & 9TRRE were based close to our camp and so it was sometimes the case that a raw sapper from one of these other camps would visit our barracks to meet up with a friend or colleague. It was not the first time that such a sapper, when entering the camp would be stopped at the gate by the guard commander and asked for his AB64, Parts I & II. If in order, then the NCO would give the sapper and his kit a 'good going over' and if he had not come up to scratch he'd be given a 15-20 minute period of drill. On completion he would then usually be despatched back to his camp with a flea in his ear and told not to appear at No 3TRRE in s**t state again. There was no respite from the 'bull'.

Naturally, we seemed to have parade after parade. Passing out Parade, GOC's Parade, Remembrance Parade, Exercise 'Knockout', Queen's Birthday Parade, and I think, on one occasion a Battle of Britain Parade. For these events everything had to be 'tickety boo' - especially so for the annual GOC's parade. On completion of the parade there would be a complete tour of the camp by the General Officer Commanding the Aldershot Garrison - a Major or Lieutenant General. On these tours he would look at anything and everything that took his fancy and you had to be very alert to be able to respond to his questions or requests. 'Sods Law' dictated that he would pick on one of your sappers - usually the least bright spark in the firmament - and question him on some arcane topic regarding his training. You could only keep your fingers crossed and hope that the sapper wouldn't let the troop down. The GOC's inspection would last the whole day, and, as far as I remember, end up with either a dinner or a cocktail party in the mess with him in the evening. These were days that the CO did not relish, as any shortcomings would be his responsibility. As it so happened, the two such inspections that I was involved with, both as a sapper and as a subaltern, went very well. The CO was very well pleased to be complemented by the GOC at the end of the day.

'Exercise Knockout' was another of these all day affairs. Having experienced this exercise as a sapper in basic training I was well aware of the attention given to the exercise from the CO down. This was not surprising since the reputation of the camp and the CO depended, to some extent, on our collective performance. As I have recounted previously, the scenario proffered from Southern Command was that a nuclear strike had hit the south of England and that all the regiments in the Aldershot Garrison Area had to be on full alert ready to empty the whole camp at 30 minutes notice. Assembling a whole regiment that could be dispersed over a large training area was some task. Fortunately, we were told that it would happen sometime within a given time frame of about two weeks. So every troop within the camp had all kit prepared and assembled ready to be 'kitted up' and entrained onto TCVs for transportation to some unknown destination. Naturally, we prepared well by having several dry runs. Nevertheless, it still got very fraught, as no one wanted to be 'tail end Charlie' and let the regiment down. As it so happened on the actual day the regiment was not as dispersed as it might have been, and so assembly, entraining and reaching our allotted destination was achieved within the allotted timescale - just. Everyone was delighted, and I seem to remember that any non-essential duties were dispensed with for the rest of the day.

Perhaps the success with 'Exercise Knockout' had made everyone a bit more relaxed. A few days later we were out on the training area demonstrating to the sappers how to use the various explosives that they may encounter, and possibly use, at a later stage in their service.

For these demonstrations each of the NCOs would take a small group of sappers and show them how to prepare and detonate various types of charges such as the 'Beehives', 'necklaces' and the like that I had encountered earlier in my basic training. Naturally, each group was at a considerable distance from the others as the effects of some of the devices could be quite spectacular. One of the more mundane demonstrations was to show the sappers how to crater a road, airfield runway, or similar, to restrict an enemy's movement capabilities. This meant coring a bore into the ground to a depth sufficient to cause the size of crater that was required, and then packing the bore with the amount of explosive required to do the job. Penetrating the explosive was the detonator with the attached detonating cord, which sent the detonating spark to the detonator; and then 'Bingo', you had your crater, or bloody great hole in the ground if you had overestimated the amount of explosive required. After the explosive, detonator and detonating cord had been placed, the bore had to be backfilled and tamped exceeding carefully so that the detonating cord, or detonator, did not become detached from the explosive; or worse still, if over tamped, could prematurely ignite the whole damned thing. One could carelessly wipe out a whole troop, your self included, if care was not taken - something the authorities took rather a dim view of…

So it was that on this particularly warm day I toured around all the demonstrations to make sure all was being done correctly, and it was, that is until I came to lance corporal X's group. Wally was demonstrating how to crater a large hole in a road or runway and I arrived just as he was tamping the borehole which was charged with explosives. Because we were running a little late Wally was being more that a little cavalier with the tamping and I had to intervene pronto before the worst happened. This was not like Wally because he was a good NCO, but clearly he was having an off day, something not advisable when handling explosives. I mentally noted that I would have to speak to Wally later about the incident but in the meantime the situation in hand had to be dealt with. I then got him to finish the demonstration and move onto the detonating phase with everyone at a safe distance from the projected crater. And then came ignition - or rather it didn't come. My worst fears had been realised. Wally had either detached the detonating cord from the detonator, or the detonator from the explosive. In these situations it then falls to the troop officer to resolve the problem and make the situation safe. There was nothing for it but to wait for the mandatory 30 minutes to see if the charge would ignite before attempting any further remedial work. It did not ignite after the 30 minutes, so remedial action had to be taken. Another hole had to be cored alongside the failed charge and then another suitably sized charge inserted and primed to detonate both sets of explosives. Coring the bore was a two-man job using a hand auger because of the fact that the initial charge had been placed at some depth to create a spectacular end to the day's training. Naturally, Wally felt obliged to volunteer to help me core the bore so that I could place the new charge. Although I was reasonably sure that there was not going to be a delayed explosion, the situation was still fraught with tension until the new explosive was in position and the bore had been tamped. This time there was no mistake, the 'whole bang shoot' went up, and it was really quite spectacular. An initial large charge, together with the extra, but slightly smaller secondary charge, created the sort of show that got the sappers fully excited. It was a good end to the days training as it demonstrated the effects of crating; and the consequences if things were not done correctly, although that latter scenario had not been part of the original training schedule. Later, when I got Wally in the troop office on his own, I gave him a bit of an earful. He swore never to be so careless again. I suspected he wouldn't be as he was still a good NCO.

It was sometime around this period that 'Taff', our communist leaning civilian batman got thoroughly enraged with Rusty and I. As was the case each morning 'Taff' would do his rounds of the rooms within the officers mess dispensing an early morning 'cuppa' for the junior officers. Well, this brew out of a very large teapot was a thoroughly disgusting mixture; at least Rusty and I thought so. Consequently, each morning after 'Taff' had left our room one or other of us would empty the teacups into the sink, which we had in the room. This all went well until the morning 'Taff' discovered what we had been doing. He was beside himself with rage. Why did we not like his tea, de dah, de dah, de dah? In his most diplomatic of tones, and Rusty could be extremely diplomatic, and was up there with the best of them, he explained that it just was not our thing. 'Taff' was not at all amused. It was several days before he regained his composure and would speak to us again. *Bloody national servicemen* he could be heard to mutter for a few days afterwards.

As demob was fast approaching it was time for me to delegate one of the last extra mural duties that I had acquired early in my posting to 3TRRE. It was that of being in charge of the Regimental Small Bore Shooting Team. The duty was not onerous and I soon found a 'fall guy' to take on the responsibility. In the months that I had been in charge I had - in the main - enjoyed it. The bonus was that if any of the 'sharpshooters' in the squad were unable to compete in any of the various inter regimental competitions I was able to stand in as a substitute. I was just good enough to classify myself as a reserve team member. Fortunately, no one ever implied that I was pulling rank.

The end game

It would appear that I have concentrated on incidents outwith what would normally be called military duties. Perhaps that is because the duties themselves would be rather boring to relate although they were no less demanding in spite of that. And of course there were the other tasks that one got called on to carry out, such as organising the cocktail party for the OC's Squadron bash. The particular one that I remember was going to be held on the island in Hawley Lake - weather permitting. It had been suggested by a few of us that it would be an unusual venue and a good one, assuming the weather was kind. It therefore seemed obtuse to some of us subalterns that we got the 'fun' part of organising the do, including making all the arrangements for the decorating of the island and the transport there and back - yet strangely enough we did not seem to figure so highly when it came to drinking with the guests. Odd, we thought! Still, we managed to consume our fair share of the refreshments.

But clearly, our days in the sun were slowly drawing to a close. One by one our comrades were getting demobbed. Yes, they were being replaced by new 'subbies', but it was our friends and comrades that we had been so close to and with whom we had gone through training and so much 'bull s**t', that we were losing. One by one they went. First Bill B, that was a good and well organised 'leaving do' at the Frensham Ponds Hotel. There were many a sore head after that one. Then John F. John, who had introduced me to Sibelius, was also a good yachtsman in his own right. He had taken me on many a sunny Sunday afternoon onto Hawley Lake to enjoy the delights of a lazy day sailing in the sun. And there were other friends as well. As was the custom in the mess there was always a 'Blues' dinner night when an officer was about to be demobbed. With the large crop of second lieutenants leaving just before I was being demobbed there was many a morning when sore heads were in abundance.

Then it was Rusty's turn because he had been conscripted a month before I had. A few weeks prior to his demob he took the remainder of the two weeks leave due to him. By this time most of the others had departed to civilian life. It was a long two weeks in the mess with all the old buddies gone. One bright spot to liven up the proceedings was the annual Farnborough Air Display in mid September, which was held only a few miles from our barracks. Since two of us were rather bored that weekend, John J and I decided to have a trip to the air show. It was rather spectacular with all the latest kit on display including the state of the art rocket at that time - *Blue Knight* and the latest surface to air missile *Bloodhound.* But my one particular memory regarding the air show was the sound of the jet engines, or rather the volume of sound. Particularly the decibels emanating from a Lightning jet fighter as it swooped low over our heads and then started a steep climb engaging the afterburner to power the engine as it did so. John and I were directly under the plane when it started its climb with the afterburner fully engaged. The decibels were so great that we had to cover our ears; such was the pain being at close range to the sound. The flames shooting out of the back of the jet engine were equally spectacular.

To add to the boredom I had volunteered to do 'orderly dog' duties over a 'Block Leave' weekend, and so the camp was strangely quiet and, unusually, there were no urgent call outs or incidents. Time hung very heavily indeed. I had even sold my bike to my replacement – second lieutenant Dick R - for the same sum that I had bought it - £5. And, as I recall, it was to him that I also sold my Blues Dress Uniform, as he was of a very similar size and build as myself. Why he did not have a No.1 Dress Uniform I do not recall.

When Rusty returned from his two weeks leave he had less than a week left to serve. Those last few days we spent in deep conversation well into the small hours reminiscing and deciding what life was going to be like as a civilian once again. The most renowned opening lines in twentieth century literature sprang readily to mind:

Let us go then, you and I,
When the evening is spread out against the sky *

It was clear that we were ready for life on the outside, and I had the added advantage of going back to Lorna, who by this time had found a flat that we could rent for the first phase of married life. No more gut retching moments on Waverley Station saying goodbye until the next leave. As the days slipped by I had a couple of letters from Rusty who was now living the life of a civilian once more. In the latter letter he told me that he had managed to book a plane ticket to Bombay - his home city - and that he would be leaving on the 10th October 1959. He said he wasn't sure if he would return to the UK; it all depended on the job opportunities that might come his way. I reflected somewhat gloomily on whether our paths would ever cross again; such was the comradeship that could flourish when teams and groups experienced the 'ups and downs' of service that we had seen.

In retrospect we had been a very varied bunch of subalterns. Tony P and Dick B were both architects. John B was an atomic scientist, Jim M a philologist in Celtic Studies and John F a geographer. Bill S was a manager from ICI and Rusty was a manager who went on to be a main board director of an International company. As for myself I returned to be a consultant civil and structural engineer. There were others as well including, Frank W and Bill B our two 'petrol-heads', but regrettably I have forgotten their occupations.

I had already lined up a job with my former employer some months prior to my demob so it was straight back to work within a few days of my return to civilian life. And so in October 1959 two years national service drew to a close in a very low-key manner.

The days in the sun were over. It was now time to return to a normal civilian life.

* T. S. Eliot ; The Love Song of J. Alfred Prufrock ; 1915

EPILOGUE

By the early 1970s Lorna and I were well settled into married life and by now had two young girls; a third was to arrive later. As was our custom then we had rented a flat in or near London to have a short vacation in the summer in the Capital, something we enjoyed. On one such visit I decided that Lorna and the girls would like to see Guillemont Barracks where I had served nearly two years of my life. So, armed with a road atlas we headed off to Farnborough and Cove. The road atlas was needed because by this time the area was criss-crossed by new roads and a motorway. However, I soon found Guillemont Barracks, or what remained thereof. All that was left was the tarmacadam barracks square - everything else had been erased from sight and memory. *Is that it,* came the withering reply from the two young damsels in the back seat who were clearly not impressed. And as it so happened, neither was I.

After demob Rusty and I exchanged Christmas cards on a regular basis, but with the passage of time that eventually fell by the wayside as these things do. It was only when I retired and acquired a computer that I began to wonder what had happened to Rusty, and where was he now? This was in the very early days of the Internet and I had only just acquired a modem to allow me to access the World Wide Web. This was a top of the range modem that operated at 14,000 bps. At the time this was state of the art, or nearly so, but in reality it operated at the speed of cold treacle on a winters morning; and you paid for every minute online. Nevertheless, I started my quest to try to find him. My known contacts with him up to that time were Bedford, then Lebanon and then Hong Kong, where I thought he had operated in a managerial capacity with some airline, or with something to do with the airline industry. Try as I might I could not track him down. I searched every known avenue that I could think of, but without success. The search was frustrating to say the least because I had been looking on and off for many years without any success. Then one day about eleven years into the search I got a breakthrough, or so I thought. He, as far as I could see was employed by Air India in a very senior capacity. Then, by dint of further searching, found that he had been Director for Air India in Europe for a number of years before returning to Mumbai (Bombay) to have a seat on the main board. But still I could not pin him down. I even tried to search the online telephone directories for Mumbai (Bombay). I started, but could not complete the search using this avenue; it was just far too bamboozling to say the least. Then, in year twelve I got another break through, but again, just when I thought I had nailed him, I still could not get any contact details. It was frustrating to say the least. Then again in year thirteen I got yet another lead. This time I got a lead through his old public school magazine, which I had chanced upon, more by good luck than anything else. Through this link I was ultimately able to make contact with Rusty and tell him of my endeavours to track him down. It was great to be back in touch once more. Rusty has eschewed the Internet and email, but every three or four weeks he phones me from Mumbai and we have a brief chat. It transpires that when he was transiting between India and Europe to take up his post as the Air India director in Europe that he lost all his belongings in a major fire in one of the luggage holding areas at Geneva Airport. Thus, he had lost my, and everyone else's contact details, which accounted for the breakdown in communications many years earlier. Sadly, after he retired Rusty had a bad accident when in France and so his health is not as good as he would have liked it to be, but at least we are now back in touch once again.

Some years after retiring I happened to chance upon another ex comrade living in Edinburgh, who had been at Gordon Barracks when I was there. When he got commissioned he told me he had been posted to Germany. As he related, one of his rotational duties was to have a spell in charge at one of the checkpoints on the Berlin Wall during the height of the Cold War. It was the case that each troop fulfilling this task had to be well presented because their Russian counterparts on the other side of the checkpoint were always immaculately turned out. He said it was with some alarm that he discovered shortly before going on duty that he found that he had left his khaki tie back at camp. A quick 'ask around' of his troop at the checkpoint proved fruitless - there were no spare ties to be had. So, the ever-resourceful Patrick cut the tail off his khaki shirt and fashioned a more than reasonable lookalike that passed muster on the day. The 'Ruskies' would have been quaking in their boots if they had known how resourceful the enemy was! He had a bit of explaining to do to the Quartermaster to get a new shirt.

The most common question posed to former national service men is, *do you regret having to serve two years national service in the military?* The answer to that question depends on how the serviceman approached his service. Some 'skived' and tried to dodge everything they could. Their reply to the question was usually *a complete waste of time.* Others, who enthusiastically embraced the two years duty thought otherwise. One former colleague who served in Cyprus thought it the best two years of his life.

Frank Sinatra phrased it rather nicely:
Thanks for the memory
Of things I can't forget,
...
How lucky I was.

As for myself, if I'm ever asked the question I'm very firmly in the camp of 'The Little Sparrow', Edith Piaf:
Non, je ne regrette rien
(No, I regret nothing).

Such are the inconsequential memories of two years serving 'Mrs Windsor'. Sepia tinted memories now.

APPENDICES

The Corps Song of the Royal Engineers

'Hurrah for the CRE'

The Corps song of the Royal Engineers, *Hurrah for the CRE*, originated among RE units during the South African War (Boer War; 1899-1902). The words, partly in English and partly in Zulu, are sung to the tune of the traditional South African song *Daer de die ding*. The Zulu words are a complaint that as there is too much work for too little wages, and too little food, they are leaving.

Good Morning Mr Stevens and windy Notchy Knight,
Hurrah for the CRE.
We're working very hard, down at Upnor Hard,
Hurrah for the CRE.
You make fast, I make fast, make fast the dinghy,
Make fast the dinghy, make fast the dinghy.
You make fast, I make fast, make fast the dinghy,
Make fast the dinghy pontoon.
For we're marching on to Laffan's Plain,
To Laffan's Plain, to Laffan's Plain.
Yes we're marching on to Laffan's Plain,
Where they don't know mud from clay.
Ah, ah, ah, ah, ah, ah, ah.
Oshta, oshta, oshta, oshta.
Ikona malee, picaninny skoff.
Ma-ninga sabenza, here's another off.
Oolum-da cried Matabele,
Oolum-da, away we go.
Ah, ah, ah, ah, ah, ah, ah.
Shush ... Whow!

Glossary for the Corps Song

Mr Stevens:	Chief Clerk of Works.
Windy Notchy Knight:	Warrant Officer in the School of Military Engineering.
Upnor Hard:	RE training area on the River Medway near Chatham. Still used at the present time.
Lafflan's Plain:	RE training area near Aldershot. Named after Captain Lafflan RE.
Ikona malee:	Too little money.
Ma-ninga sabenza:	Too much work.
Picaninny skoff	Too little food.
Oolum-da:	Native working chant.
Ooshta:	Another native working chant.

The Royal Engineers' Drinking Song

There are a great many more verses to the song than those listed below.
New, and more up to date ones are added from time to time.
Many verses have lyrics that are inappropriate to list in print –
much depends upon the state of inebriation of the songsters at the time of rendition.

We Are The Engineers

Godiva was a lady, who through Coventry did ride,
To show the royal villagers her fine and pure white hide.
The most observant man of all, an engineer of course,
Was the only one who noticed that Godiva rode a horse.

Chorus:
We are, we are, we are, we are, we are the Engineers,
We can, we can, we can, we can, demolish forty beers,
Drink rum, drink rum, drink rum all day, and come along with us,
'Cause we don't give a damn for any old man who don't give a damn for us !

She said, "I've come a long, long way, and I will go as far,
With the man who takes me from this horse and leads me to a bar.
The man who took her from her steed and lead her to a beer,
Was a bleary-eyed sapper - a Royal Engineer.

Chorus

A maiden and an engineer were sitting in the park,
The engineer was working on some research after dark.
His scientific method was a marvel to observe,
While his right hand held the figures, his left hand traced the curves.

Chorus

An RE sapper once found the gates of Hell,
He looked the devil in the eye, and said, "You're looking very well".
The devil looked right back at him, and said, "Why visit me ?
You've been through Hell already; you went to No.3 !"

Chorus

Rapunzel let her hair down for two suitors down below,
So one of them could grab a hold and give the old heave-ho.
The prince began to climb at once, but soon came out the worst,
For the engineer rode up a lift, and reached Rapunzel first.

Chorus

In 1887 at the battle of Waterloo,
Napoleon was hoping that Josephine was being true.
But while Napoleon was fighting from the front and at the rear,
Josephine was taken by a Royal Engineer.

Chorus

In Rourkes Drift South Africa, the year we won the war,
Zulus said lay down your arms or we will kill you all
Not bloody likely came a shout from the rear.
The only man to stand his ground was a Royal Engineer

Chorus
We are, we are, we are, we are, we are the Engineers
We can, we can, we can, we can, demolish forty beers
Drink rum, drink rum, drink rum all day, and come along with us
'Cause we don't give a damn for any old man who don't give a damn for us!

No.3 - 3 Training Regiment Royal Engineers

PLANS

3 Training Regiment Royal Engineers
Guillemont Barracks
Cove, Hampshire
Circa 1957-1959

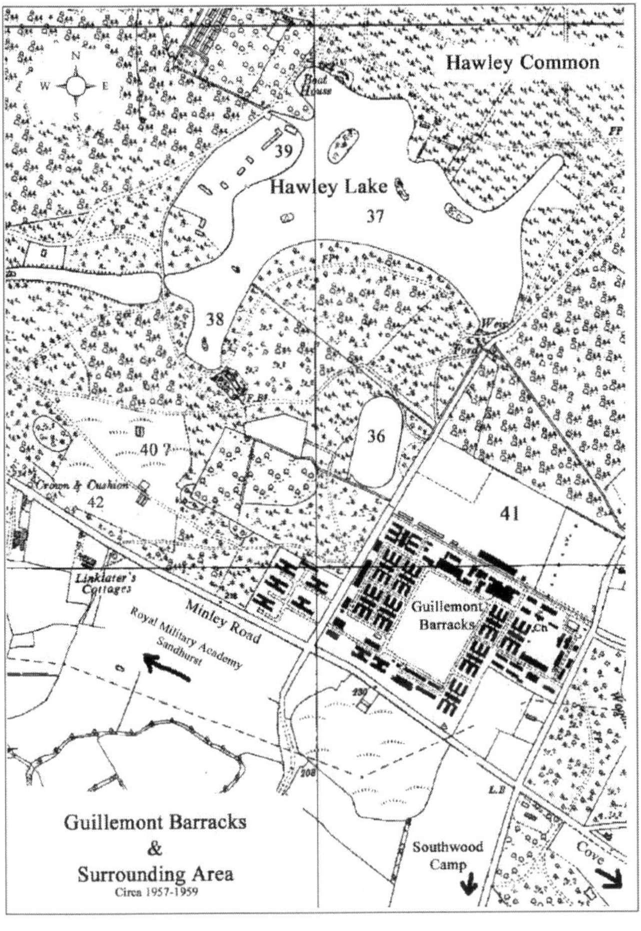

Guillemont Barracks
&
Surrounding Area
Circa 1957-1959

Legend for Plans of Guillemont Barracks

Guillemont Barracks
Circa 1957-1959

1. Officers' Mess
2. Officers Sleeping Quarters
3. Chic's & Rusty's Room
4. Officers' Mess Garden
5. Officers' Garages
6. Assault Course ?
7. Main Gate.
8. CO, 2IC, Adjutant, R.S.M
9. Guardroom
10. Gymnasium
11. Laundry & Bedding Store
12. 'B' Squadron Spider
13. 'A' Squadron Spider
14. OR's NAAFI
15. NCO's NAAFI
16. Barber's Shop
17. Tailor's Shop
18. Military Transport Depot
19. Cookhouse
20. Armoury (REME)
21. Indoor Rifle Range
22. Regimental Chapel
23. PRE OCS
24. Detention Centre ?
25. Education Offices (RAEC)
26. Medical Centre (RAMC)
27. C' Squadron Permanent Staff
28. RHQ Offices
29. QM Stores
30. 'C' Squadron Office
31. 'B' Squadron Office
32. 'A' Squadron Office
33. Drawing Office/Architect
34. WO's & Sgt's Mess
35. Brick Air Raid Shelters ?

Guillemont Barracks
& Surrounding Area
Circa 1957-1959

36. Athletics Track
37. Watermanship Training
38. Bailey Bridge Training
39. Dog Handlers Compound
40. Armoury & Explosives Store ?
41. Rugby & Football Pitches
42. Crown & Cushion Pub

These locations are the best the collective memories of the author and Ian Chappell can provide after the passage of nearly sixty years.

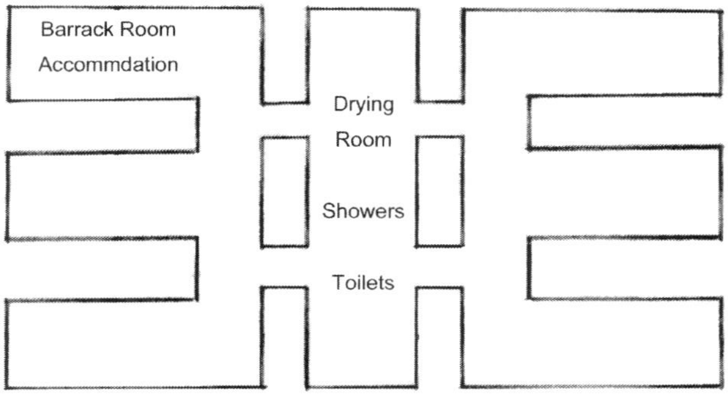

Layout of a Typical Spider

This layout has been reconstructed from my memory of nearly sixty years ago, consequently, it is not necessarily an accurate representation, particularly regarding the scale of the various internal areas.

PHOTOGRAPHS

RHQ Offices comprising: CO,2 I/C, Adjutant, RSM & Chief Clerk

Basic Training 3 TRRE, October 1957. Author RH end of middle row

Mons Officer Cadet School, February 1958. Author 5th from RH end of back row

Commissioning Troop, Brompton Barracks, June 1958
Author centre back row

Commissioning Parade, Brompton Barracks, Chatham, June 1958
Author being inspected

307 Party, 'B' Squadron, 3TRRE, Guillemont Barracks, Cove. June 1958
2Lt Charles Husband, subaltern on the left. 2Lt Dick Cox, subaltern on the right.
My first party. I was taking over from Dick Cox who was being demobbed

313 Party 'Passing Off' Parade, 'B' Squadron, 3 TRRE. October 1958
From the left: OC 'B' Squadron, 2Lt Charles Husband, Major General ? from the Aldershot Garrison

313 Party 'Pass Off Parade', 'B' Squadron, 3TRRE, October 1958
2Lt Charles Husband, Party Officer

? Party, 3TRRE, Guillemont Barracks, Cove. September 1959
2Lt Charles Husband, subaltern on the right; 2Lt Dick Reid, subaltern on the left.
My last party. Dick Reid taking over from me as I was about to be demobbed.

Bailey Bridging at Hawley Lake

Launching Bailey Bridge at Hawley Lake

Small Pontoon Bridge at Hawley Lake

3TRRE Rugby Team - Quarter Finalists in Army Rugby Cup - Circa 1958/59

Back Row : ? , ? Thomson, ? ,Quartermaster SM Bill Greenwich , ? Swann, ? , Cpl ?

Middle Row : ? , ? , ? John Hart, ? Salmon, ? , ? Robinson

Front Row : Cpl Bob Taylor, 2Lt B N Rustomjee, Lt Col Brown, Malcolm Staines (Captain), Capt John Goodson, 2Lt Ian Maddox, L Cpl Derek Hann

Officer's Cap for Battle Dress and No.2 Service Dress

Officer's Collar Badge for No.2 Service Dress

Badge for Royal Artillery similar,
but only 7 flames from grenade,
not 9 as above

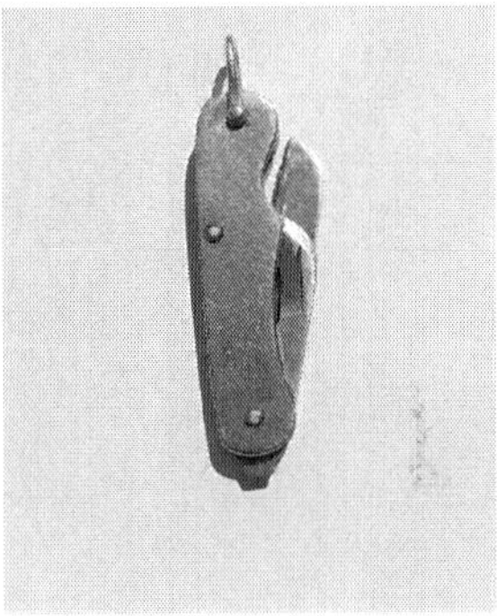

Other Rank's Jack Knife

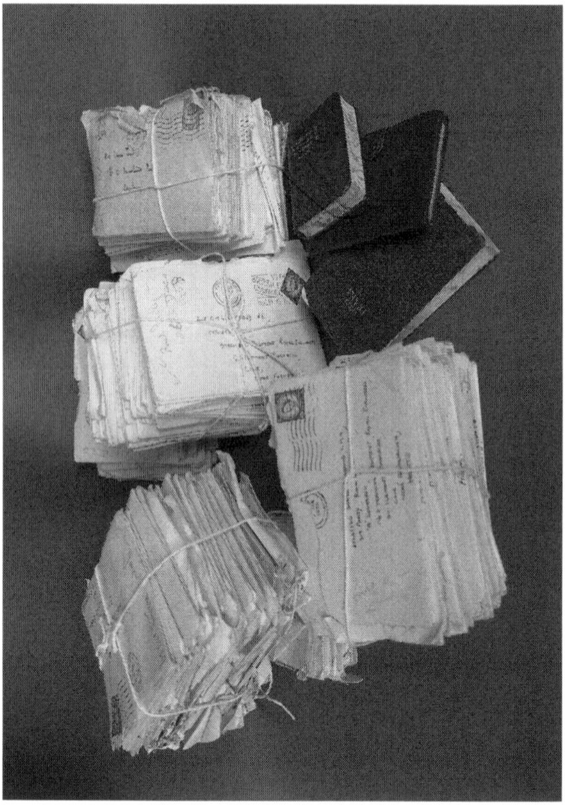

My Archive of Letters and Diaries

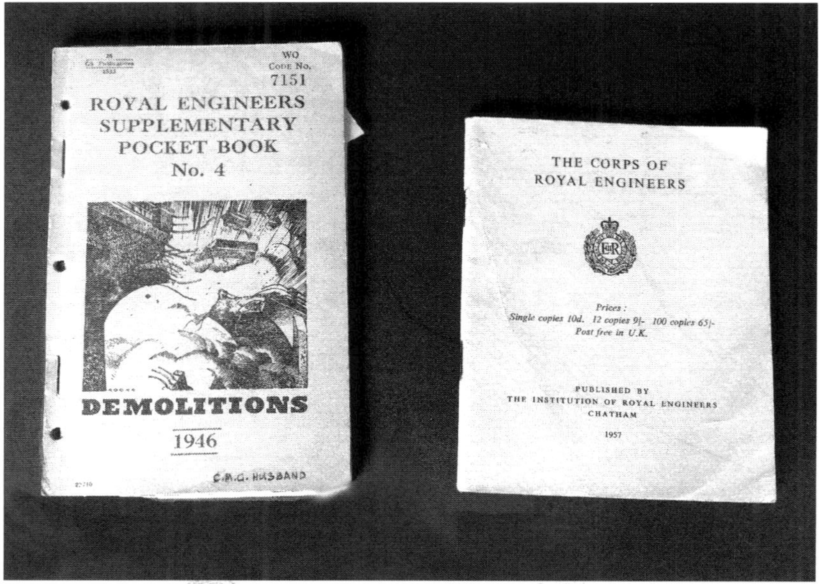

Royal Engineer Pocket Books – the only ones I still possess

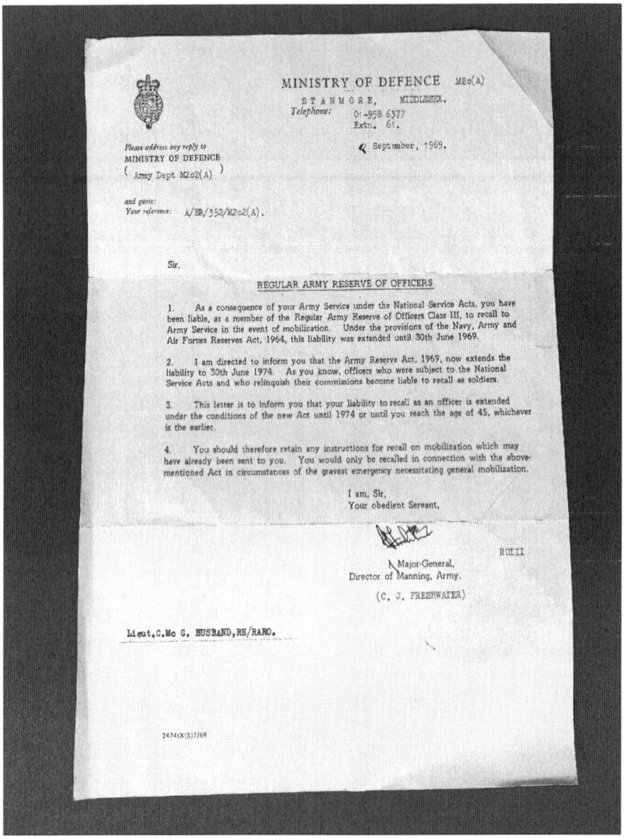

MINISTRY OF DEFENCE M2c(A)

STANMORE, MIDDLESEX.

Telephone: 01-958 6377
Extn. 61.

Please address any reply to
MINISTRY OF DEFENCE
(Army Dept M2c2(A))

and quote:
Your reference: A/ER/352/M2c2(A).

4 September, 1969.

Sir,

REGULAR ARMY RESERVE OF OFFICERS

1. As a consequence of your Army Service under the National Service Acts, you have been liable, as a member of the Regular Army Reserve of Officers Class III, to recall to Army Service in the event of mobilization. Under the provisions of the Navy, Army and Air Forces Reserves Act, 1964, this liability was extended until 30th June 1969.

2. I am directed to inform you that the Army Reserve Act, 1969, now extends the liability to 30th June 1974. As you know, officers who were subject to the National Service Acts and who relinquish their commissions become liable to recall as soldiers.

3. This letter is to inform you that your liability to recall as an officer is extended under the conditions of the new Act until 1974 or until you reach the age of 45, whichever is the earlier.

4. You should therefore retain any instructions for recall on mobilization which may have already been sent to you. You would only be recalled in connection with the above-mentioned Act in circumstances of the gravest emergency necessitating general mobilization.

I am, Sir,
Your obedient Servant,

RCIII

Major-General,
Director of Manning, Army.

(C. J. FRESHWATER)

Lieut.C.Mc G. HUSBAND,RE/RARO.

2474(X(S)7/69

Letter from Ministry Of Defence re Army Reserve List

GLOSSARY

Adjutant
The officer in charge of the administrative duties of a regiment or battalion. Also responsible for the discipline of junior officers. Usually carried the rank of Captain.

ASAP
As soon as possible. In military use - now!

AWOL
Absent without leave.

Battle Order
The webbing worn by a soldier preparing to go into battle which comprised a lesser amount of webbing than that for full Field Service Marching Order, but which normally included the small pack, ammunition pouches, strapping, rifle, bayonet, helmet, ground sheet, and water bottle.

BD
Battle dress, which from WWII to the end of national service, was fashioned from a rough khaki coloured serge material that had all the properties of smooth sand paper. It also had excellent water retention properties making it the least suitable material under the sun for exposure to the rain or weather.

'Block, The'
The Detention Centre or Regimental Prison. Bare brick cells within a secure compound run by the Regimental Police. It was a forbidding place of no beauty. Discipline was extremely strict and prisoners were not allowed any clothing or equipment that would aid a suicide or escape bid, e.g. knives, forks or laces in boots etc.

Cadre
A small select group of troops chosen to undertake further advanced training. Normally as preparation for promotion to the next rank above their present status.

CB
Confined to barracks, the slang term for which is 'Jankers'.

'Champ, The'
The unofficial name given to the army ¼ ton truck made by Austin.

Officially known as Truck ¼ ton, Austin. It was the British army equivalent to the American army Jeep.

'Dear John'
A letter from a girl friend or loved one at home stating that she was terminating the relationship.

'Eating Irons'
Knife, fork and spoon. These implements were supplemented by a tin mug and two rectangular tins or containers - one large and one small. These containers, known as mess tins, acted as plates to hold your meals.

'Fizzer'
A slang term for a disciplinary charge.

FSMO
Field Service Marching Order. The full set of webbing worn by a soldier, which varied from decade to decade, but would normally comprise the following:
Large back pack, small front pack, belts and shoulder straps and cross straps, two ammunition pouches, water bottle holder & water bottle, bayonet frog and gaiters together with helmet, rifle and ground sheet, which also doubled up as your outer rain wear.
The small pack contained all the equipment to survive for 24 hours including mug and mess tins. The large pack contained most of the other kit, except for your second battle dress.
Non-essential kit and other large items, or personal kit that could not be carried within the packs above was carried in a kit bag.

GD
General duties.

'Get some in'
A term used to imply superiority over another colleague; mainly applied to length of service.
When disembarking from a troop ship for example, the lead soldier might turn to a colleague behind him, and as he stepped off the ships walkway onto the foreign soil, he would turn and shout 'Get some in', referring to foreign service.

GOC, CO, 2IC, OC

General Officer Commanding; the officer in charge of a garrison or similar, comprising more than one Brigade of troops; usually of Major General rank and above.

Commanding Officer; the officer in command of a regiment, or battalion, of troops. Normally a Lt Colonel.

Second in command; the deputy to the Commanding Officer, or the second in command of any group of troops.

Officer Commanding; the officer in command of a squadron, or company, of troops. Normally a Major.

HARP

High Altitude Rocket Projectile. A low explosive rocket that could be fired over distances of one third to half a mile, or thereby, to bridge large gaps or ravines in difficult terrain. Attached to the rocket would be a light rope, which in turn, could be used to pull over another heavier rope to allow a large gap to be bridged; and thus allow equipment etc to be transported across the gap.

Hershey Bar

A popular milk chocolate bar, normally only available in the United States.

'Jankers'

See CB.

'Kip'

Sleep.

Lafflan's Plain

A training area used by the Royal Engineers for demolitions and other activities. Located near Aldershot.

'Lance Jack'

A slang term for a lance corporal who wore one stripe on each arm. An NCO.

MO

Medical Officer

NCO

A non-commissioned officer who could be any rank between Lance Corporal and Staff Sergeant, or the equivalent.

OCS
Officer Cadet School

OR ***or*** **Other rank**
A reference to military personel who do not hold a commission.

'Orderly Dog'
A slang term for Orderly Officer, or Duty Officer.

PDQ
Pretty damned quick, or, in military parlance:
pretty damned f*****g quick. Meaning - now!

Pick helve
The sturdy wooden shaft or handle which was inserted into the metal head of a pick or axe.

'Pit'
Bed or bunk.

Port arms
The command to present a rifle from the position of attention so that the bore of the rifle can be inspected for cleanliness. The command is triggered by the inspecting officer tapping the barrel of the rifle with a cane or pace stick. When the inspection was undertaken by an NCO during basic training it was legend as to the varieties of debris that they could claim to see within the barrel; extending from birds nests to bird s**t, and much else besides. When this happened one could expect to be put on a 'charge' with all that that entailed.

QARANC(S) or QUARANC(S)
Queen Alexandra's Royal Army Nursing Corps

QM
Quartermaster

RAEC
Royal Army Education Corps

RAMC
Royal Army Medical Corps

'Red Caps'
A slang term for the Military Police who wore a red cover over their service dress cap.
During the years of national service they patrolled the mail line railway stations in London assiduously to waylay any serviceman whose turnout did not meet their high standards. Kings Cross and Waterloo Stations were their particular favourite haunts due to the concentration of troops in Southern Command moving between camp and home. It was wise to be on the alert when passing through these 'hot spots' otherwise a 'fizzer' might be your lot, with all that entailed. You would certainly be detained long enough for you to miss your train connection.

REME
Royal Electrical & Mechanical Engineers

RHQ
Regimental Headquarters

RSM
Regimental sergeant major. A senior non-commissioned officer. Usually of Warrant Officer Class I grade.

'Sapper initiative'
The innate initiative that a sapper, or any rank within the Corps of Royal Engineers, was expected to have, and to exercise, when confronted with a problem outwith the normal run of events. Within the Royal Engineers one could expect to be confronted with a multitude of situations for which there was no textbook answer.

SAS
Special Air Service.

'Stag'
The slang term for a shift when on guard duty.

TCV
Troop carrying vehicle.

'Tinkers mufti'
Civilian clothing worn by military personel. It was often referred to in derogatory terms.

TRRE

Training Regiment Royal Engineers.

In the mid - late 1950s the four training regiments for the Royal Engineers were; 1TRRE at Merebrook Camp, Malvern; 3TRRE at Guillemont Barracks, Cove; 6TRRE at Deville Barracks, Southwood Camp, Cove: and & 9TRRE at Morval Barracks, Southwood Camp, Cove. Deville Barracks and Morval Barracks were adjacent to each other, and collectively known as Southwood Camp.

Guillemont and Deville were named after two of the battles of the Somme in WWI.

'Tuttie fruity'

A type of sweet fruity flavoured confectionary bar, normally only available in the United States.

Upnor Hard

A training area used by the Royal Engineers on the banks of the River Medway near Chatham. Still in use at the present time.

'Weekend finger'

If you have to look up this definition you need to 'get a life'. Make an educated guess!

WOI & WOII

A senior non-commissioned officer of rank Warrant Officer Class I, or Warrant Officer Class II, with a WOI being more senior than a WOII.

A regimental sergeant major would normally be a Warrant Officer I.

The regimental sergeant major at the Royal Military Academy at Sandhurst is now designated Academy Sergeant Major, and is one of the most senior warrant officers in the army. In recent times, the rank of Army Sergeant Major has been introduced to designate the army's most senior warrant officer.

WOSB

War Office Selection Board. A selection board of senior officers that would overview the selection of candidates deemed suitable to undertake training as a commissioned officer.

The selection board lasted four days and selection did not mean a commission; merely the entry to the officer cadet training course, which would last another six months, and where a candidate could be failed at any stage of the training.

UNOFFICIAL MILITARY ACRONYMS

These acronyms were first started during WWII and continued in use during the years of national service. They were normally printed in upper case letters on the reverse side of an envelope sent from a serviceman to his loved one back home.

There are two categories of acronym:

Group I
Those printed on a normal exchange of letters.

Group II
Those printed on a letter being sent immediately prior to some leave being taken.

Do not read any further if you are sensitive to profanity.

Group I:

SWALK:	Sealed With A Loving Kiss
ITALY:	I Trust And Love You
EGYPT:	Everything's Great You Pretty Thing

Group II:

EGYPT:	Eager To Grab Your Pretty Tits
BURMA:	Be Undressed and Ready My Angel
NORWICH:	(k)Nickers Off and Ready When I Come Home
POLO:	Panties Off and Legs Open

You were warned!

FURTHER READING

Alford, Richard (Editor)
To Revel in God's Sunshine
1981

Baxter, D.
Two Years To Do
Elek, 1959

Chambers, P. & Landreth, A. (Editors).
Called Up. The Personal Experiences of Sixteen National Servicemen, Told by Themselves
Alan Wingate, 1955

Findlay, D.
Stand By Your Beds!
Cualann Press, 2001

Fowler, David
National Service, Elvis & Me!
Farthings Publishing, 2009

Forty, G. A.
A National Service Scrapbook
Ian Allan, 1980

Hafferty, M.
Get Some In : One Man's Memory of National Service
Digory Press Ltd

Hickman, T.
The Call-Up. A History of National Service
Headline, 2004

Johnson, B. S.
All Bull. The National Servicemen
Allison & Busby, 1973

Royle, T.
The Best Years of Their Lives. The National Service Experience 1945-1963
Michael Joseph, 1986

Thorne, T.
Brasso, Blanco and Bull
Constable & Robinson, 2000

Vinen, Richard
National Service : A Generation in Uniform : 1945-1963
Penguin Books Ltd, 2015

War Office
Drill (All Arms)
HMSO, 1951

War Office
Infantry Training, The National Serviceman's Handbook
HMSO, 1951

ABOUT THE AUTHOR

Charles Husband is a retired consultant civil and structural engineer.

After completing his college studies and an indentured apprenticeship as a civil engineer he was conscripted into the army for two years national service, as was the requirement in the late 1940s, all of the 1950s and into the early 1960s. During this period of service he was enlisted into the Corps of Royal Engineers where he trained as a sapper during basic training before being selected to train as an officer in the same corps. After being commissioned he served as a training officer within Training Brigade of the Royal Engineers.

On completing national service he returned to civilian life to work as a consultant civil and structural engineer.